a diverse
NURSE
THANKS VIETNAM

A STORY OF LIFE, LAUGHTER, LOSS, AND LOVE

Published in the UK in 2021 by Diverse Publishing

Paperback ISBN 978-1-7398707-0-6
    eBook ISBN 978-1-7398707-1-3

Typeset by SpiffingCovers

a diverse
NURSE
THANKS VIETNAM

A STORY OF LIFE, LAUGHTER, LOSS, AND LOVE

SHÂN ELLISON BARKER

This book is dedicated to all the hard working
people within the National hospital for
Tropical Diseases in Hanoi, with love and thanks
for all their amazing care

Enjoying my time as Miss Jersey Battle of Flowers 1973

*The time I pressed the fire extinguisher
instead of the stop button*

PROLOGUE

"Never give up! No regrets!"

This was my family motto to my boys, and has been my personal motto throughout my life. It's the thing that has kept me going through my extraordinary experiences as a nurse and a British airways stewardess, and the trials, tribulations and humorous sides of life. I had two sons along the way, which was the best thing I have ever achieved after six miscarriages. It seemed I must wait until the age of 40, and then after all those miscarriages they arrived one after the other!

I was born in Liverpool and lived in Crosby until I was nine when we moved to Caldy in the Wirral, Merseyside. My father was a Liverpool pilot on the River Mersey and my mother was a nurse at Liverpool Royal Infirmary. My eldest son is a pilot, but in the skies, and my youngest son lives in Vietnam. I love to challenge myself, and enjoy sailing and motor racing, and something funny always happens when I do…like the time I was motor racing in a Formula Four car at Brands Hatch. After finishing the race, overtaking as many cars as possible, I pulled in at the paddock…and pressed the fire extinguisher by mistake to stop the car and covered this beautiful machine in foam – to the embarrassment of myself and my eldest son. My heroes Christian Horner and Stirling Moss would not have been amused…or maybe they would have been!

I now live on an island called West Mersea in Essex. It's strange how history repeats itself. My mother met my father when he was a patient in her hospital, and the marriage ended in divorce. And I met the father of my children in hospital. He was my patient when I was a nurse, and our marriage also ended in divorce.

Covid-19 hit Italy early in 2020, and who would have known as I sat inflight reading a fashion magazine, and my partner John reading the headlines of a Vietnamese newspaper, that the magazine and newspaper would play a significant part of our six weeks in Hanoi. Just a few days before there had been excitement, giggles and chinking of glasses and cheers as I celebrated my birthday at home with John (Dixon), my eldest son Sam, and some of my friends before we set off to Vietnam to see my younger son Chris. How normal it all seemed, and how life and everything we barely gave a thought to would change within a matter of days…

Some of the names have been changed to protect the privacy of the people in the story.

Sunday 1 March 2020

After six months of planning, and three weeks of deciding what to pack, at last our one-month holiday to Vietnam and Cambodia had arrived! We were booked on flight VN54 from Heathrow, and John and I were very excited about the trip. We'd saved hard, upgraded to business class, and the first thing we planned to do on board was celebrate with a glass of champagne! Tom, our cool local taxi driver, arrived in a rather swish Mercedes, and we were on our way!

We had to be honest, the first-class lounge area at Heathrow was rather disappointing – the anaemic-looking sausages were certainly not very appetising! – but hey, a good spicey Bloody Mary did the trick, and then it was time to board. I noticed the very obedient sniffer dogs, one looking remarkably like my dear dog Monty, and I told John about the time, after a long walk with some girlfriends, and having stopped to have a drink, I'd tied Monty to a wooden table outside the cafe. When I went back to my car I called him, forgetting I had tied him to the table, and around the corner came my obedient dog dragging the long, oblong table behind him – and looking exhausted and bewildered. I was sure these dogs were as well behaved as Monty; after all, he was from the Sandringham estate.

We flew from Heathrow, somewhere I had flown in and out of hundreds of times in the seventies and eighties when I worked for British Airways on the 747 aircraft.

We showed our passports and were asked if we had

been Italy recently, to which I replied, "No, but if we had what would happen?" and the curt reply from the check in person was, "You would not be permitted to board the aircraft."

It was great to turn left when we boarded the Vietnamese Dreamliner 787 – especially after all those years turning right down the back of the plane working with BA – and we were greeted with a glass of champagne by the beautiful Vietnamese staff in their turquoise dresses, just like I had worn as my summer uniform in 1975. They were wearing masks, and I mentioned to John that they wouldn't protect anyone directly from the Covid-19 virus, which was just making headlines, but they would help with less contamination. I had been an operating theatre nurse for 20-odd years after my stint with BA, so knew all about mask-wearing, and remembered a particular surgeon saying that he'd seen more infection from not wearing a mask during surgery than he wished to reveal. He explained they were for our protection as well as the patients, and decreased the risk of contamination from blood spillage, or even if someone had a cold, but were ineffective after an hour or so. (Much later I found out that at this time there were just 11 cases in Vietnam, 220 in the UK, but many more in Italy.)

We made our way to our seats, 5f and 5j which were on each side of an aisle. I didn't sit down straight away, and stood sipping delicious champagne – well, I was gulping actually, as I considered myself already on holiday, and if I could have another glass before take-off that would be just lovely.

Being a friendly soul, I said hi to the two passengers behind me, who I must say were rather scruffily dressed; but they were obviously going trekking, as we had done last September on the west coast of Portugal. They were not friendly at all, to the extent that I felt embarrassed I'd said hello. I looked away, and there was the captain looking down the almost empty cabin smiling at me, so that was fine. Looking at him made me think about my eldest son Sam, a captain on a 737 and always happy. He's often the youngest person (on the staff) on the aircraft, and a passenger once said to him, "You only look about twelve!" and he replied, "No, I'm actually twelve and a half." The passenger apparently looked ready to jump off!

Sam had always wanted to be a pilot, in fact his very first word was "plane". He'd told a teacher this one day, after a debate about an exam he had thought was "pointless". His headteacher had said, "We all want to be a pilot, Sam…" Years later he saw the very same headteacher in a supermarket. Sam was in his captain's uniform, and the headteacher saw him but Sam did not say hello to him, because he is simply not a show-off. (Personally I think he should have spoken to him to show him that anything is achievable.) He'd done his first solo flight on his sixteenth birthday and he was a natural, so relaxed, and his father and I were so very proud of him. He failed his driving test the next year though, but at least he could fly a plane, and solo no less!

Anyway, John said "Cheers!" and we carried on sipping (I was still gulping) our champagne. John whispered to me that the Vietnamese lady next to him on his right in 5k did not look well and had a horrible-sounding cough, but I was too happy with my champagne to comment. (When I look at the photograph I have of this Vietnamese passenger, with beads of perspiration on her forehead, I realise how correct John was at that moment.)

It was time to go and we sent our last text messages – me to Sam and Chris, and John to his son Joe – and buckled in. I fell asleep on board, even though it was very hot, and the food was great. The staff were really attentive. We had a very smooth landing into Hanoi.

Whilst waiting for our baggage I noticed random temperature testing going on. There was also a sign saying to report to a certain desk if you had been to Europe in the last month, but we hadn't, and the desk didn't have any passengers waiting to be seen. We collected our bags and were greeted by our guide Vinnie, arranged by our travel agent six months earlier. Vinnie would also be our taxi driver in Vietnam and onwards to Cambodia.

We checked into the Metropole hotel, where Charlie Chaplain had had his honeymoon. It was all very colonial, and we were greeted by 'Buttons' the porter – my nickname for him! The concierge said we would be unable to access our room until 3:00pm, however, which was in four hours' time. We'd been on a plane over 11 hours and needed to sleep...even though we had slept onboard. How could Trail Finders – which is an amazing travel company – not have got this organised? But then it may have been the hotel's fault. I suddenly felt really agitated, which was unusual for me as normally I'm a pretty calm and patient person, but four hours was too long. We were offered a complimentary snack and smoothie by the pool, but I would have preferred a bed...

Two hours later we were ushered to our room, and I was surprised by how tired I was considering I'd slept quite well on the plane, and we showered and got our heads down for a few hours.

Monday 2 March

Vinnie gave us a map of Hanoi and the surrounding area, and after breakfast we went out to explore, dodging the thousands of scooters. I like excitement, but death or injury under a scooter was something I wasn't willing to risk, especially in a foreign country, so we were extremely careful! We wanted to see the church, but it was closed as a precaution (the virus), which was really disappointing, so we continued dodging the scooters and explored a bit more, but we did not have much energy. I had been very bloated that morning. I was also really pale, and wondered if it was just jet lag (we were getting older...!), or something I'd eaten. As we were walking my stomach seemed to bloat even more, so much so that John patted my stomach whilst we were wandering down a narrow alley and asked how the baby was doing. I looked down and, horrified, saw that I looked about ten months pregnant! A local lady saw him pat my stomach and did the sign of the cross and smiled. Well, miracles do happen... (I am 67 and John is 73!)

I suddenly remembered I had not got enough of my HRT with me and mentioned this to the concierge when we got back to the hotel. Within an hour I got a call to say it had arrived, which stunned me. Here we were in Vietnam, and yet an hour later I had the prescription I needed. I wondered how long it would have taken my local surgery to get it in…certainly not an hour!

We had dinner that night in a fabulous French restaurant, where a bottle of water was the equivalent of £10! But we figured we were on holiday and not to worry too much. I remembered my son Chris saying that in south Vietnam it was the equivalent of £15 for an entire meal where he lived.

Tuesday 3 March

After another delicious breakfast at the hotel – we were spoilt for choice! – Vinnie collected us and we made our way to the incredible university complex to admire the modern architecture. We also went to the Confucius-inspired Temple of Literature, which has exhibits on the various clans in Vietnam, and I started to experience excruciating stomach pains, just like the miscarriages I'd had in the past, and twice had to run to the toilets. I didn't want to say too much to John, as I always seemed to be ill when we landed at a new destination, and I really did not want to lose our baby…

Anyway, we walked through the old French Quarter, with the streets named after trades, like Silver Street, and it was all so organised, which surprised me in such a chaotic city. Further on a dishevelled-looking lady was selling T-shirts with 'Good morning, Vietnam!' on them (after the film starring Robin Williams) for only $4, and she was also begging for food. I wished I could buy the whole lot off her, but you know what men are like about shopping, so I quickly bought one with the few dollars I had on me, with John and Vinnie walking on ahead.

It started pouring with rain, and visibility became really poor, which was a real shame as we were just passing Ho Chi Minh (the revolutionary Vietnamese leader and president) Mausoleum, which is known locally as Uncles' Mausoleum due to the intimate and friendly atmosphere the leader created wherever he went.

A profound moment for us was weaving our way down an alleyway to visit a local family (there were six people living in the three-metre by three-metre rooms). A beautiful woman greeted us, with her mother by her side. They were both immaculately dressed, and their home, which was made of bits of corrugated iron and fragments of wood, was also immaculate. To make a living they cooked soup which they sold in the mornings.

We had dinner downtown in a place called Nha Hang Ngon, 26 Tran Hung Dao Street, which was a bit like eating in Tokyo, with pictures of the food in the windows. The food was all freshly cooked and John ate for England – pork, beef and crab rolls, and two massive carrot juice drinks (to keep the Big C away)!

On the way back to our hotel we walked past the British Embassy, where they were displaying a poster of the sixth festival of Portmeirion in North Wales. We had been there the year before, and it had been great fun watching Rag and Bone Man and many more talented artists, and laughed that we should come all this way and the picture be on display. Little did we know that the Embassy would become a big feature of our trip.

Wednesday 4 March

John was feeling lethargic, as was I, but we went to visit the opera house in Hanoi…which was also closed. Again we were really disappointed, but appreciated that they seemed to be taking precautions against the virus here. (When we watched the UK news it seemed nothing was being done over there and the cases were rising.)

We had an unusually disappointing Vietnamese meal downtown, and then went back to our hotel. A brilliant live jazz band was playing so we stopped to listen. There were two American lads on the table opposite us, with two Vietnamese girls, and they were having a hoot! I wondered if they were high-class girls who they'd brought in for a good time…they were having fun, believe me!

We had a couple of cocktails and then went down to the best stocked bar I'd ever seen, where we met a couple from Suffolk who owned a boat called *Susie* – and we had a couple (or was it three…?) more cocktails. How could I refuse!

Thursday 5 March

I woke up feeling very tired, but then I had had one (three) cocktails too many the night before! A pretty waitress greeted us for breakfast – it was very busy – and asked us if we would mind sharing a table with an elderly couple. The gentleman had paralysis on one side, and as I suddenly spied a table for two in the conservatory I declined. This was fortuitous for him, as you will see later on in this story.

We were being collected by Vinnie at 8.45am, and said goodbye to the hotel as we would be starting the next part of our trip today. I had a photo taken with the bell boy, Buttons, and could only imagine how proud his mum was of him in his immaculate uniform. And so she should be. Soon I would be seeing my son, after two years so, as much as we'd enjoyed Hanoi, leaving meant I was coming closer to seeing him.

Vinnie drove us down to Halong Bay to board a boat to the floating village. We stopped at a pearl shop on the way and I purchased some face cream for my wrinkles – that looked like crevices as deep as the grand canyon. But I was so tired. If only I'd had the energy, like I'd had when I climbed and camped in the Grand Canyon for 10 days a few years back to raise money for breast cancer, I think I would have been enjoying these trips more.

We set off again, and I started dozing in the back of the car. Vinnie was pointing things out to us as we drove, like the rice fields, and he must have been surprised at our lack of enthusiasm. It wasn't that we weren't interested, we were both just so, so tired and kept falling asleep.

We decided to miss the first tour of the village and went straight to bed when we got onboard our junk boat, *Jasmine*, barely aware of the gorgeous deluxe cabin with a balcony I had booked for us. It was not like me to miss something we had paid for. We both blamed the cocktails and hoped we'd feel better after a nap.

We then joined in the BBQ lunch onboard, with all my favourite seafoods like crab, sea bass and massive prawns! It was delicious. We went up on deck to take some photos, but the view was actually very disappointing, not at all like in the 1977 James Bond film *Tomorrow Never Dies* – but then we discovered that the movie was filmed in Bangkok, Thailand, because negotiations to film in Vietnam had fallen through. That would be it then...

We got up early to join in the tai chi which was happening on deck, but we weren't very good and ended up giggling at how hopeless we were – we had no coordination! It reminded us of when we tried to learn ballroom dancing at the yacht club in Mersea, where John and I now live. We proved rather a challenge for our tutors as we giggled so much then, too, and all we learnt was the box step, and I'm not sure I can even remember that step now!

After our nap and a great lunch we finally had some energy and went to visit the caves around the spectacular protruding rock formations on a little wooden boat. Our guide was a young boy who was full of fun and as excited as I was when all these delightful little monkeys joined us on board, giving us the cutest smiles for the bananas we had brought with us. Chris told me they're considered a pest though, and can be vicious as they know that if they nip you you'll drop whatever food you're holding and they can grab it. The monkeys were hopping around the rocks like ballerinas…old Rudolph Nureyev had nothing on them!

Back onboard the magical *Jasmine* we enjoyed our last night with a candlelit supper of more sea bass and tiger prawns. They were cooked on our table, and my imagination ran away with me about ladies dressed in beautiful gowns being served by immaculate waiters ready to fulfil our every whim. Mind you, it wasn't far off for us, just minus me in a beautiful gown!

But we suddenly started feeling light-headed, and we looked at the amazing spread, embarrassed that we could hardly eat anything. For me to refuse food, especially fish, is unheard of. And John, who is of a stocky stature, always teases me and says I can eat more than him, which is true. I've always had a good appetite and I told him the story of when I'd arranged to have two dinner dates with two different doctors when I'd been at Jersey General, one at 6.30pm and one at 8.00pm. The first date picked me up outside the front entrance of the hospital and we went to the Capannina restaurant for a lovely meal. He'd dropped me back after the meal, and I ran down the corridor to the nurses' entrance to meet my second date, and guess where he took me…the Capannina restaurant. We even sat at the same table! The waiter had been funny: "Feeling hungry tonight, madam?" (I recently returned to Jersey to celebrate 50 years since I started my state registered nurse training and the restaurant was still there! What a hoot we had reliving the days of our training. We were still all the same, laughing nonstop remembering our crazy antics!)

We retreated to our beds after managing to have a shower in our gold-plated (probably brass) shower, wondering what on earth was wrong with us. I don't think either of us even dared mention the *thing* – the other C word – which was taking over Europe and the UK by storm…

Friday 6 March

We were woken at 6:00am by a loud bang on the door, and then heard a nervous, shaky voice say, "Do not leave your room!" in broken English. We looked at each other in silence, and the sudden realisation that this was real, and here, was worrying to say the least.

We received no more information for three hours, by which time we were very hungry, and I searched my cabin bag looking for something to eat, but there was not even a packet of crisps. (I usually snaffle food off a plane for emergencies – a throwback to my days with BA.)

A voice on the other side of the door then told us to pack our bags, but we had anyway, as that day we were due to go to the airport to fly on to Hue.

Another two hours later there was a bang on the door and we were ushered off the beautiful *Jasmine* with three other people and put in an ambulance. Vinnie was in the distance, leaning on the harbour wall and looking shocked.

After a five-minute ride we arrived at Thaison Hotel and were greeted by six or seven people dressed in white 'space suits' standing on the steps and holding guns. They sprayed us from head to toe in some kind of disinfectant. My heart was pounding, and I kept looking at John. This was like a scene out of a sci-fi movie, and I felt scared. We were escorted up the stairs to our rooms, which had guards outside, and I noticed a large sign on the door with a long list of quarantine rules.

Once we were inside the room a voice came over the Tannoy system: "Do NOT leave your room." Another space suit-clad person – it was impossible to tell whether it was male or female as all we could see were the eyes through the goggles and not a single word was uttered – and indicated with arm movements that we should lie on the bed. I was pushed flat by one of them, who was holding a swab in his/her hand, and shoved it straight into my mouth and then up my nose like he was swabbing my brain. (No wonder it seemed to take forever…!) When it was John's turn I heard a horrible sound coming from his throat, like he was gagging, and suddenly I had a flashback to the passenger sitting to the right of John in seat 5k on the plane and the ghastly sound of her cough…

By now we were absolutely starving and raided the small fridge. The only food in there were miniscule boxes of Pringles, which we devoured in seconds. I was tempted to drink the brandy, but I've always found it a bit strong. Exhausted and hungry, we fell asleep, only to be woken by phone at 5.00am. We were instructed to pack our bags and leave our room in half an hour as we'd tested positive. I took my temperature – being a retired nurse I always carry my mum's old thermometer with me wherever I go – and eek! it was 38.8!

I phoned Chris, who we were supposed to be visiting soon in South Vietnam, to say we may need to rejig the trip a little as it was possible we would have to quarantine for two weeks.

We were escorted to an ambulance, with cameramen outside, and were put in the back with a couple from Harlow. The man was a retired police officer. The front of the ambulance was screened off with plastic, and the sirens were started as we screeched away from the hotel… and again my heart started pounding. Nothing much was said, and we had no idea where we were going except that it would be a hospital, and in a great hurry, overtaking the overloaded wobbly scooters with startled people darting out of our way as the siren continued nonstop.

Two and a half hours later we arrived at a hospital for tropical diseases in Hanoi and were escorted into the building by more people in white suits. I lay down on a trolley at the entrance, by now feeling exhausted and ill and unhappy, and we were wheeled to an emergency ward and blood was taken. We were also x-rayed and given vitamin pills. I can't remember what they were, and wondered why, but felt too ill to care. They brought us some food, but it was awful, and by now I couldn't have eaten if I'd tried. Our inmates were a friendly guy called Richard who, believe it or not was a steward with British Airways, and a woman called Trudy whose husband was on another floor. There were two Vietnamese people in the next cubicle. We did not see the people from Harlow again.

Monday 9 March

Two very long and hot days and nights had passed, with some of us feeling more and more ill. The two Vietnamese in the next cubicle were replaced by two English guys, who were coughing horribly. John contacted our insurance company.

I had no appetite, and wasn't able to eat the hot, sticky Vietnamese rice they kept bringing us. Trial Finders sent a food hamper, which everyone was really grateful for. John was able to eat as he was not displaying any symptoms.

By now I was struggling to comprehend what was happening around me, and am now writing from the notes John scribbled in his notebook and memories of conversations and events we discussed later on. I was coughing so much that I was sent for an MRI scan. I felt like I had crushed glass in my lungs, my temperature was 39 degrees and my pulse 102.

Tuesday 10 March

It was on this day 45 years ago that I'd joined British Airways as a stewardess on the 747 fleet and began a job that would be an absolute dream – and a scream. What a way to celebrate, in Hanoi Hilton...

I'd loved nursing, but I was yearning for adventure. I'd had a Peruvian boyfriend when I was 17 and so wanted to go to see his country, but it turned out British Airways did not even travel there! At my convent boarding school (I was not a boarder) there were girls from all over the world, and that had also whetted my appetite. The interview for BA had been tough, but walking in the high heels I had borrowed from one of the nurses had been tougher! One of the lady interviewers was horrible, and by the time I got up to leave the interview I did not want to join BOAC. When she asked me what I would do if I did not get in I said, "I'll join British Caledonian." It turned out I was the only person to get in that day (later I heard that only one of four thousand applicants were accepted), and despite the horrible interviewer, I was on cloud nine!

I went on a jumbo jet for the first time on 19 March 1975 and, wow, it was enormous! Very different from the propeller Viscounts when I commuted to Jersey! We had to practice going down the slides and deploying the life rafts. This was such fun, to the extent I nearly went flying off the side. There were shark repellents in the safety packs, and if we were doing the arctic routes there were down coats with furry hoods! We were shown where the black box was kept, which is in fact orange. It sits at the back of the plane in one of the bulkheads – the safest area. It always tickles me to think that the passengers who pay the most sit in the most dangerous seats…but then again there are not many plane crashes, which brings to mind the doctor at my medical asking me if I had any distinguishing marks. When I said no, his shocking answer was, "Well, you will not be identified in an air crash then." How lovely!

We would fill the teapots with Moet Chandon and drink it on landing – the passengers thought we were drinking tea! – and fly to amazing places, like Jamaica, where we visited Dunns River Falls, where I felt I had arrived in paradise. We came from all walks of life so there was always something to talk about, and the room parties were incredible. We filled our flasks up with booze on the plane, which continued for many years until BA decided enough was enough and anyone caught stealing booze was immediately sacked! It was also the end of free coffee and food too. We were allowed one BA biro in our bags now, and that was that. Fair, I suppose. When I look back now I feel quite ashamed, but at the time it was what most of us did.

I started to get some Bahrain flights, and I loved these as they were a great earner. It was known that one of the sheikhs threw huge parties in his palace on the beach, and gossip flew about that if you saw a specific-colour car in the crew car park then a stewardess must have slept with him as this was the typical gift he would give her afterwards! After a couple of trips we got invited to the palace, and two huge cars arrived to take us there. We all sat around the perimeter of a vast gold room with a huge picture of the Queen on the wall. It was all so glamorous, but it felt soulless in there, despite the champagne and jewels and silk clothing. (We still enjoyed the champagne, though!)

Lying in my cubicle in hospital felt like many years from the palace in Bahrain. Others were chatting around me, trying to make each other smile, but they were very worried. I was the only one who was ill. John was now testing positive, as we all were, but still had no symptoms.

Being ultra-sensitive to good and bad vibes, I noticed a sudden feeling of coldness when a new couple walked into the ward. I looked closer and couldn't believe it: it was the scruffy, unfriendly couple who had been sitting behind us on the plane. And yes, they ignored us again. But then the woman – her name was Maisie – decided to come over and chat, and started complaining about the conditions on the ward. I advised her not to say such things, but there was no keeping her quiet. Everyone in the hospital was doing their best, and of course the sinks and toilets could have done with a few bottles of bleach, but the care we were receiving under the circumstances was amazing.

Wednesday 11 March

Another day of nasal swabs and Dracula coming for more blood. I felt so ill, but remember hearing that we were soon to be taken upstairs to the sixth floor, which was the 'positive floor' but for patients who were not so ill.

Richard was a funny guy, and made us all laugh when

a nurse came round for our laundry. He'd given them his underwear, which had been returned dark brown and would have fitted a three-year-old perfectly, so I decided not to part with mine! (The laundry service stopped shortly after that.) As the others chatted I remembered a flight to New York, when I found a rather large pair of ladies off-white pants in the toilet at the back of the plane. I can hardly believe that I did this now, but I paraded them up and down the aircraft asking if anyone had lost them! Some of the passengers were in hysterics, as were the crew, but of course no one owned up to them being theirs. How I did not get the sack I do not know, as I was summoned weeks later at Heathrow to see one of the BA bosses, who reprimanded me. The lady who owned them had complained!

That afternoon an elegant Vietnamese lady was put in a cubicle three beds from me on the right of my bed, and then two very important-looking men dressed in black arrived with a TV crew and started to film and speak to the woman. We were all very intrigued. Who was she?

The others were taken away for scans by people in space suits. I looked at the clock. It was 5.00pm. I was amazed at how fast the time was going when all I was doing was lying in my bed, and recording my fluid output on the chart at the end of my bed, just like my nursing days except that now I was the patient. How was it that I'd ended up in bed coughing, and with what felt like fragments of broken glass in my lungs, when I should have been exploring Vietnam and visiting my son?

Where had this virus come from? We were told almost nothing as barely anybody spoke English, and we had no TV or newspapers, so the minutes kept ticking by as the people in space suits came and went. It was impossible to tell whether they were doctors, nurses or cleaners as they passed by.

The demon nurse with the nasal swab, who smiled a lot – with her eyes – came by again, and I imagined she had a really great sense of humour and we would have got on very well…in different circumstances. I certainly needed a sense of humour every time she came anywhere near me with that evil swab.

We were given fly swats as the flies were now horrendous, but I didn't have the energy to move and couldn't swat them. I spent the day under my sheet, coming up to drink the Ensure energy drinks we had been sent by the travel company. It was the only thing I could stomach, and even though they were full of sugar I made sure I had three a day.

I wondered if I would soon feel better. I was still on oxygen and attached to a monitor. I could see my pulse, and watched it getting faster…and then suddenly I started to feel worse than I had ever felt in my life. My nurse's instinct kicked in and, in horror, I realised I was rapidly deteriorating. I started gasping for breath.

Thursday 12 March

I thought I was dying. My breath was very shallow, and I could see my oxygen levels on the monitor were down to 80%. I could feel my pulse pounding. I was hooked up to an ECG machine, which kept sounding its alarm, but no one came.

I could hear snippets of conversation. Apparently the patient to the right of me was infected by the lady on our plane – she was her aunt! She was on a drip and was very unwell. Someone said she'd handed a large bag of apples around with 'thank you' written on it before she had got so ill. Why? Thank you for what? Had I dreamt that? Through the agony of trying to breathe I looked over at her. Was I hallucinating, or did she have mountains of food piled up on her table? I hadn't eaten a proper meal for over a week. And then I saw a large mouse scuttle across the room. A doctor appeared – I vaguely recognised him as he wore heavy glasses – and suddenly he grabbed a drip stand, took off the fluid it was holding, and whack! the doctor bent down and hit something on the floor. I knew I was not hallucinating when I saw him pick it up by its tail, put it in a bag (it was still wriggling), and walk away with it.

I heard Richard say the government were now paying our medical bills. How did he know that? And was it true? I later found out it was true.

At 5.00pm I was taken for another MRI scan and a chest x-ray.

John called my sons, and his son.

Friday 13 March

John: 'The virus is attacking Shân again. She was taken for yet another scan but collapsed as they put her in a wheelchair. She is so thin her pyjamas were falling off her. I'm scared. It's hell watching my love suffer.'

Saturday 14 March

There was almost no communication, just "Hold out arm" as more blood was taken and more intravenous solutions were given. Then a nurse with a wheelchair arrived and, one by one, John, Richard and I were taken in the lift up to the sixth floor. There had been monitors everywhere on the emergency ward, yet this tiny room only had three beds and nothing else. The fact that there were no monitors made me feel uneasy. I was still not breathing easily.

The next thing I remember was feeling very dizzy as I was wheeled to the x-ray department for yet another MRI scan. I was then put back in emergency. I'd not even said goodbye to John or Richard. How would they know where I was? And how would I find out how they were? I don't remember much else that day except that Maisie, the unfriendly passenger, was in the bed opposite me and seemed to be trying to talk to me. Perhaps she was mellowing, or I was still hallucinating.

The doctor with the glasses came in and I heard him say his name was Doctor Thang – he later became a very important person in my life. What he said next, in his broken English, chilled me to the core: "You last words?" Why had he said that to me? Or was he talking to another patient? There were four people in their space suits around Maisie's husband's bed, with a trolley covered in green sheets, and I was aware of his legs being tied to his bed with rags. (It was like a scene out of the TV programme *MASH*.) Maisie was staring at him, and – bumphhh! – they inserted an intubation tube. I will never forget that scene as long as I live. This intubation procedure is not always straightforward, as I remembered from my nursing days, and it was all over in a second or two, with nothing further being said.

John: 'Shân now on electrolytes.'

Sunday 15 March

The same doctor, Doctor Thang, came to see me in between my long coughing episodes and asked me if I would like to try an antiviral HIV drug as an experiment as it may help me improve. I asked if the culprit's (from the plane) aunt had taken it and he said yes. I knew she was still very poorly, and for once in my life I did not act impulsively. I asked what the side effects were, and he said vomiting, so my mind was just about made up. I cannot bear vomiting, whether it's me or anyone else, which is why I worked in operating theatres where anti-emetics are given before surgery. If a patient is sick, no problem, it just gets sucked away along with all the other fluids.

I asked him if I could think about it for 24 hours.

Monday 16 March

John: 'Shân wrestled with what to do through the night and decided not to take the antiviral drug for HIV. She felt that if she started vomiting that would definitely be the end for her. She is so weak. She now has pneumonia so has been given antibiotics for seven days. She also has a very itchy rash on her back and is very, very uncomfortable.'

Tuesday 17 March

Richard said there are now 57 cases in Vietnam, 46 more than when we landed in Hanoi.

John: 'Very bad night. Shân is so uncomfortable, but her temperature is down and she's coughing slightly less. Am so worried. Spoke to Sam in the UK and Joe again. She has a really sore bottom, so I asked for Sudocrem but don't know if they will find any.'

And later: 'Shân's lungs badly damaged. On oxygen all night. Told Sam to cancel Tom (the taxi driver) for 29 March.'

I didn't think I would be going home at the end of the month, and probably not ever, and started writing on my top bed sheet. I remembered that with British

Airways if it wasn't held down, and could be of use…
but best I don't elaborate on that. BA, what a long, long
time ago… One face kept coming to mind and I wrote
his name on my sheet – Whizzer – but I'm not sure why. I
just knew I was very, very sick, and my sheet became my
comfort, the thing I could record my random thoughts
on… (Sam would later call it my Bayeux Tapestry.)

'Whizzer' Williams, the scouser purser, was such a
hilarious guy. (I was born in Liverpool, and most scousers
are!) He would ask for the passengers' tickets on boarding
and clip them as if they were boarding a train, and if they
were in seat 46k at the rear of the plane he would say,
"Oh, that's where the Queen sat last time," and they were
so gullible they believed him. He did get into trouble
though. We were flying over Lake Erie and Whizzer got
on the PA and said, in a deep scouse accent, "We are
flying over the dirtiest lake in the world." Unfortunately, a
passenger in first class had just been in charge of cleaning
it! Whizzer did not get the sack but was reprimanded for
that. As was I, if you recall, for parading the large pair of
pants down the cabin! I still can't believe I did this, and
nor could the Queen Mother when she found me trying
on her hat and said, "It suits you"!

On the approach into Heathrow, after the captain
had said his bit in his BBC voice, Whizzer would often
pipe up and say, "If you're sitting on the right of the
aircraft, the lady holding the watering can at Windsor
Castle is our Queen." I'm not exaggerating when I say
that all the passengers would lean over to the right as
far as they could to look out of the windows. If the seat

belt sign had not been on, and they had not been in their seats, I swear the plane would have veered sharply to the right!

Poor Whizzer. I met him many years later in Kuala Lumper for breakfast, and his wife – 'the dragon' as he used to call her – had left him, and it really knocked the stuffing out of him. I never saw him again after that. In those days we had to retire at 55, so I guess he'd left BA soon after.

Maisie was moved from the emergency ward and I remember thinking I would miss her, and perhaps she wasn't that horrible after all. She was the only one near me who spoke English, and even changed my bed sheet for me. This was something we were supposed to do for ourselves, but I was too weak to do anything. I could not even walk to the end of my bed without struggling to breathe.

I was the only person in my cubicle now and I felt very alone. The culprit's aunt was now in the next cubicle and still very ill. And I remember a young Vietnamese boy vomiting – he had been given the HIV drug – and I never saw him again.

By three o clock in the morning I was on two drips, and my arms were black and blue. My heart kept stopping, and the alarm was continually going off, but still no one came. How could they not hear the alarm? Was anybody there? I could just see the monitor, and could see my oxygen levels were still very low.

Then I saw three or four white-suited men at the bottom of my bed. I realised they were discussing ventilating me. My nursing training kicked in again – thank goodness it did – and when I was asked "Can breathe?" by a female nurse I hadn't seen before I lied and said yes. When they left I struggled to get onto my left side, knowing that this helped my breathing, and managed to stabilise my heartbeat. I started to count the tiles on the ceiling to stay awake – alive? – and stay on my side. I remember thinking I must send some flowers to Tricia, because she'd texted me to say my lungs were damaged after I'd sent her a picture of them. She said I would never run a marathon, but who cared about that? She helped me, though, and I never forget people who are kind. I thought about my great great grandma, who had lived to be 102 years and seven months old, and was so healthy. To get anywhere near that, and be even half as healthy, would be good.

That night was long. I felt so weak, but strangely not scared, even though I thought many times I might now be dying. How could this be happening? I was on holiday, the trip we had planned for so long… I knew John would call my boys. My boys… I was confused. Where were they?

I started thinking about them, and remembered being really pregnant, huge, and the boys' father taking me to Fakenham racecourse as he had a photography job there. He was really worried I would go into labour on the way and found a sleeping bag and put it in the back of the car, which had made me laugh. I was really hoping I wouldn't have the baby in the back of the car but I appreciated the gesture. The horse racing began, and I was watching closely to see if my £1 bet on a horse would come in, and started jumping for joy when it went into the lead. The lady standing next to me asked me when the baby was due, and I said, "Last week." Her face was a picture of horror! It reminded me of the famous painting 'The Scream'.

I kept reliving their births. I remember I was induced when I went over my due date by ten days with Sam, and nearly gave birth in a wheelchair running up the corridor to the labour ward asking for an epidural, but it was far too late for that! I stayed in hospital for six days, and after three days Sam still had not cried, so I asked the nurse if he was OK. "Of course," she said, "he's just a calm baby, but I can make him cry if you wish?" After a slight slap on his bot – wow! – his lungs opened up! To this day Sam is still as laid back as ever. We had thought Chris might be a Downs baby, as he had an enlarged head and I was high risk being 41. I was worried I wouldn't be able to love another child as much as I loved Sam. I think lots of mothers pregnant for the second time worry about this, but when he arrived – after a disastrous attempt at a pool delivery – he was in a poorly state but turned out to be just fine, and I loved him just as I loved Sam. He was one ounce lighter than Sam, but grew to six feet two inches. Sam is five feet 10 inches.

I drifted and counted the tiles on the ceiling and stayed on my side for what seemed hours, counting my heartbeats and thinking about my boys and breathing… always trying to breathe.

I really do believe that turning on my side that night

kept me off a ventilator. And kept me alive. I wondered why I hadn't thought to do this earlier, as it helped my breathing so much. I don't think I'd even had the energy to think about anything at all.

Wednesday 18 March

John: 'Shân is swabbed negative.'

I was woken up at 6.00am by the lights being switched on by the cleaner, as she always did, and I groaned "Noooo…" and she threw me a clean pair of pyjamas. She was too scared to come near me as she was not wearing a space suit, and just had a mask on and yellow wellies, but I was too weak to change into them. (Later I noted where the light switches were and, when I was strong enough, would get out of bed and switch them off again.)

My first thought was that I was alive, and my second that John and Richard were on antibiotics. I don't know how I knew this, I just knew. I've always felt a little bit psychic, and from a very young age felt different to my little friends. I remember telling my father about the flood at 23 Chetwood Avenue in Crosby, Liverpool, in 1953. The memories of the flood were very clear in my mind, and they still are now, at 68 years old, but my father would hear nothing of my story. "Impossible!" he said. "You weren't born until a month after that flood!" But I described the colour of the water, yellow-brown, and the people outside wading in wellingtons. He went quiet then. But how was it that I knew? How had I seen those images so clearly and accurately from the womb? I didn't tell him I also remembered lying legs akimbo in a big Silver Cross pram having my nappy changed...

When I was well enough, I'd been able to get to the bathroom on my own, and every day had to pee in a jug and have it weighed. I still felt so physically weak, but somehow mentally stronger – was that my imagination? – and thought I would try to get up. It was not easy doing this attached to a drip with my buttonless striped pyjama top falling open and trousers falling down, but I just about managed it, peeing in a jug and shaking my bottom (there was no loo roll, but lots of watching blue bottle flies and mosquitoes), and then dragging myself and my drip to a pair of green rusty scales from the 1950s to weigh the urine. I then shuffled back to bed. Thank goodness for the cleaner in her yellow wellies, despite her switching the damn lights on, for clearing up behind me as I dripped dry. No furniture ever got moved, but at least I had less chance of getting septicaemia.

One day when I did this I could not find the green scales, and a nurse grabbed the jug of urine I had carefully passed, pleased with myself, and low and behold tipped it down the sink! I could have cried! Funny how a little thing like this seemed so important to me.

I looked at the purple bruising on my arms from the arterial blood being taken every day, and my boobs like tubes under my pyjama top – later on, on YouTube (BoobTube!), a picture of my tube boobs would appear for all to see (no such thing as patient confidentiality in

Vietnam) – and wondered if there was a single part of my body not failing or being affected somehow by this illness. It didn't even hurt when the doctor took the blood anymore...

Once back in bed I would sink back down, clutching my diary sheet, and wonder what on earth would happen next.

Thursday 19 March

I managed to get up to go to the bathroom and looked at myself in the mirror. I looked just like my father did the day before he died. My eyes were sunken; my skin a greyish-black colour. I remembered what I always used to say to my boys when they were little, which is our family motto: "Never give up." Staring into my sunken eyes, I said to myself, "You bastard virus, you are not going to beat me." My dear friend in Sydney was battling cancer of the lungs, and she'd texted me to say, 'Don't let the virus beat you.' My mind was made up: *You're a fighter, Shân. You can do this.* I needed to see John. I hadn't known that he'd been praying for me. I had to get better.

When I went back to my bed I was told I'd had a clear swab (although I'd get another positive one at a later date). I was the only one left in my cubicle. The culprit's (now nicknamed 'the super spreader') aunt had gone. Maisie was gone. I was then told I was being taken up to the seventh floor, as it was dangerous for me to stay on the emergency ward as more positive patients were arriving. I emptied my locker of bananas and my Ensure 'survival' juice. I was so weak, but I had no help from anyone.

Friday 20 March

I wasn't moved. That morning I was told by a doctor that John's scans were not good and he was being brought back to the emergency ward. I felt relieved that at last I would be able to see him, but it was not good news about his scans, not with his already damaged lungs. (Chemotherapy had left its mark.)

But I would not see John again until 31 March, as, like ships passing in the day, I was taken up to the seventh floor in a wheelchair just as he was brought down to the emergency ward. The last time I had seen him was on the 14 March.

I looked around my new room, number 738. There were two beds with rubber mattresses, with no pillows or top sheets, just a light eiderdown. I was wheeled to one bed and left there. There was no one in the other bed. The room had its own bathroom, though. Bliss. Like a five-star hotel room to me. (Would I ever see the inside of a five-star hotel again?) There was also a window (albeit with bars on) and I could see daylight for the first time since I'd been admitted 14 days before.

I was too weak to shower, and tried to find something for a pillow. I hadn't worn any of the lovely clothes I'd brought with me for evenings out, and looked at them, and my crumpled, buttonless pale blue stripy prison-like pyjamas…

I found my phone and called John with what little energy I had. He sounded very low and was panicking about Lily…the name he calls the inoperable lymphoma behind his stomach. He has been in remission for five years, but stress is the one thing that can wake Lily, so I tried to keep John calm, telling him I was fine now so he could concentrate on himself.

It was so quiet in that room away from the emergency ward, but it felt like a prison cell, and I was shouted at every time I went to the door: "Mask on! Mask on!" I was so thirsty, and opened the fridge – it was pure five-star luxury having a fridge – and saw one bottle of water. I drank it, and put my remaining two bananas in there and the rest of the Ensure energy drinks.

I stood and stared out of the window, down at the grey concrete courtyard, glad of the daylight. I was so pleased about the privacy and the quiet, but so weak, and so worried about John.

Saturday 21 March

My darling Juan, how are you? Please be OK. I can't live without you.

I was woken at 6.00am by a bang on the door. On the trolley outside was a small beige plastic bowl with brown warm water in (it looked like old washing up water), and some noodles in a dish on the side. This was obviously my breakfast, and something I would have to get used to.

I suddenly remembered our backpack, the one with the cash and credit cards in, and John's suitcases. Where were they? I hadn't seen them since we were both moved and started to panic. Had John got them? And had I left the backpack down on emergency? I texted John and he replied to say he didn't have it or his suitcases. I went to the door to ask, but was shouted at again. It seemed the staff were petrified to come near me, and wouldn't let me near them. Peering down the corridor I noticed a water tank right at the end, so when no one was looking I shuffled down there as fast as I could and filled my empty water bottle up. There were people opposite me in other rooms, all Vietnamese and all lying on their beds just staring. The doors had large glass panels in them, with frosted strips across, so they had a little privacy, but I could still see in.

Chris messaged me to ask when we were coming to visit. He wanted to go to Hoi Ann. I told him we wouldn't be coming for a while, and that he was crazy to go. But he is young and knew best...

I ventured into the shower for my second wash in two weeks. I had a vague recollection of Maisie helping me wash when we were on the emergency ward, before she was taken away. The shower was handheld, but the feeling of hot water on my skin and just about being able to lift my arm to wash my hair – for the first time since we had been at the Metropole – was incredible. I am known for loving a long, hot shower, and really hoped the hot water wouldn't run out, but then I looked down and realised, with horror, that I was ankle-deep in murky, dirty water, and the plug hole was erupting with thick black hair, so much that the water hadn't been draining away and had regurgitated all over the bathroom floor. I grabbed some soggy loo paper and tried to pull the huge knot of hair out of the drain, and managed to remove some of it so that the water started to drain away – very slowly. (I learnt later to always remove the loo roll when having a shower!)

I didn't want to stay in there, and waded through the dirty water, ducking low as I passed the glass door with the frosted stripes on it to grab something to dry myself with – there was no towel, and there was little point going to the door to ask for one as I'd be shouted at again – and I felt like crying. I rummaged around in my suitcase and pulled a pretty white lacey top out to dry myself.

Later that morning the doctor came into my room, without knocking, and ended up with wet feet. He confirmed that my temperature was normal, and I was very happy. This continued every day, for the next two weeks, with him asking, "'Ore froat? Fever? 'Edake?" as he monitored my progress. This was the limit of his English! One day he wrote his mobile number on a piece of paper and stuck it on the wall…in case I needed him, I guessed.

For two days my room was awash with water. I was terrified of slipping and breaking a bone, and pleaded with a cleaner to bring a mop and some bleach. These items eventually arrived outside my room, and I was able to mop up the water and clean the floor. I was ridiculously pleased with myself. This was some achievement after being so ill! I then had another shower, with a clean, white, unblocked drain and, exhausted, got back into bed. It was a relief to have a shower without turning the bathroom into a jacuzzi.

Chris was still keen to go to Hoi Ann, and messaged again, but I told him I was not leaving John and couldn't leave the hospital anyway. I told him again not to go, but he was adamant that if he did get the virus he would just have mild flu-like symptoms. I told him an 18-year-old boy had just died in the UK. He would not be told, however, and kept saying I would be out of hospital soon and could make the trip to Hoi Ann. He understood I needed to stay with John for now, and asked after him every day, as did Sam, which was so sweet considering he was not their father. There was no word from John's son Joe, at least not to me, which made me sad.

Sleuth Richard texted me to say he was now on my floor, just around the corner past the nurses' station, and I was extremely pleased to hear that he was OK and that he was close by! I hadn't had a proper conversation in English for so long! He started hatching a plan on how we could meet up!

I then heard that Maisie was in a room down the corridor. I snuck out and knocked on her door, and there she was in bed on her laptop with her bags all over the large floor. She told me her husband George was on a ventilator, and looked so worried because she hadn't seen him for two weeks. I knew that feeling and sympathised. *Please, Juan, keep doing the breathing exercises I told you about...* I asked her if she had a knife, and she looked most alarmed. But I told her I fancied one of the apples that the culprit's aunt had brought in the 'thank you' bag. (Thank you, super spreader, for giving us Covid...) I needed to keep my strength up. She gave it to me, after much hesitation, and I crept back to my room before I was spotted and shouted at again.

Chris decided to go to Hoi Ann. I really did not want the stress and worry of that, as the cases were going up all the time, but he'd made his mind up. Besides, I needed to support John as much as I could, even though I could only message him.

At 10.56am my lunch was put outside the door: a lump of sticky rice and some soggy pale-green beans in a polystyrene bowl. I hoped dinner would be better, as I was starting to get my appetite back now. It wasn't. I texted Chris and he said a lump of bone and gristle and more sticky rice was a luxury. Really? He said the Vietnamese like to chew on bones. No wonder they're so slim. They had started giving me vitamin B12 though, which I was pleased about.

I opened the window to get some air in – well, as much as I could due to the bars – and to try and dry the clothes and underwear I had washed, but it just let the flies in. Great. It was so humid the clothes were not drying, anyway...

After lunch my throat was sore, so I told the nurse I needed a swab. She returned with two large swabs, the type used to mop up blood in theatres. What could I say?

Then a woman called Kathy called me from the

British Embassy, and asked me if I knew of any British nationals who wanted to go home. She seemed completely out of her depth, like she didn't really have a clue what was going on, and I decided I needed to get a bit more savvy if I was to find out for myself what was happening outside the walls of the hospital – and inside, as Chris messaged me to say one of the doctors in the hospital had now tested positive.

I got the name and number the doctor had stuck to the wall – Dr Thang – and looked him up on Facebook and sent him a friend request. I was worried this was the doctor who had got the virus, but it wasn't him, thank goodness, and later he messaged me to say John was now lying flat and on oxygen.

Maisie then messaged me to say she was being taken to emergency, but only to check if her lungs were OK. I asked her to check on John for me, and later she said he was resting. I heard that one of the women who I had met in emergency was going to be discharged soon. What? I was still in isolation? I started worrying that I'd be forgotten up here on the seventh floor. I checked my email account, but couldn't log on, which was strange. I had bills to pay, and was starting to worry about that too.

I swatted the last fly – woohoo! – and went to bed.

Sunday 22 March

Mother's Day in the UK and 96 cases in Vietnam.

Dr Thang contacted me and told me John had had

a bad night and was still on oxygen. I was so worried. I kept whispering, "Keep fighting, John, keep fighting," and imagined John trying to pull the oxygen mask off his face.

The sore throat had made me tired, and I was told it was a side effect from struggling to breathe for so long.

Maisie messaged again to say the doctors had checked on John all night. What wonderful people they were, and I felt overwhelmed with gratitude for their care in such difficult circumstances.

The floor was busy in the morning with lots of new arrivals. Breakfast arrived at 10.00am, and lunch at 11.09am. When it all died down I checked through the windows of some of the rooms. It broke my heart to see the boy who had taken us on his little boat to see the monkeys and the island. Had we infected him? I wondered how many more were ill because we hadn't known we were positive.

Richard texted me to say a TV crew had burst into his room last night, and the French guy he was sharing his room with was furious.

It was very noisy outside, and when I looked out of the window I saw some of the staff playing tennis and badminton in the concrete courtyard. What a good idea to keep fit on your lunch break. They ought to set something up like that in the UK, instead of watching TV whilst eating a sandwich.

My aunt Ann texted me to say my 82-year-old Uncle Eric had been in a car crash, but was OK. This was the uncle, my mother's younger brother, who was the first rock climber to tackle the north face of the Eiger, solo, and attempted Everest without oxygen with Habler and Messner. Maybe it was from my mother I had got my fighting spirit? My legendary Uncle Eric had had such an exciting life, and had also written a book called Life on the Edge. I remembered seeing Sean Connery in a lift when I was working with BA in Nairobi. I was on my own, and the doors opened, and in stepped Sean. I'd so wanted to say he had filmed with my Uncle Eric, but I was too shy. Eric was working on a film called "Five days one summer" starring Sean Connery. Sean mistakenly thought that although Eric was part of the filming crew he wasn't experienced in the mountains. One day he admonished Eric, saying he should be more aware of the dangerous high altitude sunrays. Several days on Leo Dickinson (Film Producer) was showing some footage of Eric soloing the North Face of the Eiger, this prompted an embarrassing apology from Connery. Bizarrely, a week later when the lift stopped in a hotel in Johannesburg, in came Sean again! Incredible! And I was still too shy to say anything!

I decided to start doing some sit ups, and managed 20 – a big difference from my usual 140, but I had to start somewhere. I love walking, and was also desperate to go for a walk to build my strength up, but was shouted at to get back in my room when I even so much as went to the door. I felt like I was in prison. I had the outfit.

Maisie messaged me to say John had asked that I contact Joe, his son. I did, but there was no reply. *Please be OK, John, please...*

Monday 23 March

I had now been at the hospital for nearly three weeks, struggled for my life, and by some kind of grace and prayers started to recover. But I was becoming paranoid. This was my third day in full isolation. Why wouldn't they let me out of my room? Food was still left outside my door, and no one would come near me. No one had ever checked if I had enough water to drink, so I still had to sneak down to the water tank and risk getting yelled at.

Joe called at 2.00am Vietnam time last night asking after his father. When I went back to sleep I dreamt about my father, and it was such a happy dream. It felt like a nightmare to wake up, despite the relief of being alive.

Another food hamper arrived, which was a godsend. It was full of bananas, energy drinks, water and M&Ms. I asked Maisie to make sure that John was drinking the energy drinks and water, but felt so, so helpless. I was still testing negative, so why wouldn't they let me see him? I did wonder if they were worried I might get ill again. In truth, I was worried about that too, but I wanted to see him and would wear a mask and anything else that was required. I hadn't heard from him directly for three days, but had texted to tell him to keep breathing, to keep fighting, and not to have the antiviral drug or be put on a ventilator.

I put the TV on for the first time in weeks after having a shower in my lovely clean bathroom. This had become so important to me, along with doing my sit-ups and appreciating every little thing available to me, like the energy drinks and the water and the daylight through the window, which I now kept closed. I felt like I was changing somehow, but then severe experiences will often do that. I was alarmed to see on Google that there were currently 106 active patients in the hospital, 46 of whom were ill, 34 of whom were Vietnamese. Later this was updated to 134 cases, but no deaths, and 17 recovering. Was I one of them?

I took Maisie's knife back. She didn't really say much to me, other than she was worried about George, who had been on a ventilator for days now. I went back to my room and jotted some more thoughts in my notebook as I had done before on my snaffled bed sheet.

Joe messaged me to ask how I was, which made me feel strong. I drank as much water as I could, and did sit-ups, thankful to God for where I was. It could have been very different, and now I had to concentrate on John and getting stronger so I could support him.

Tuesday 24 March

There were now 153 cases in Vietnam.

I'd missed four phone calls from John when I was in the shower, so phoned him straightaway. His voice was weak and uneasy. He told me he had lost so much weight and was scared it was the start of Lily waking up (the nickname we have for John's lymphoma). I told him to pretend it wasn't Lily, and to keep drinking the energy drinks. He kept asking for his passport, and seemed confused. I reminded him I had lost loads of weight too, and had been really confused at times, but was feeling stronger now and he must keep fighting. But I was in a mess after the call and started crying. I messaged John and said I could contact Barts Hospital, where he was treated before, if he wanted me to, so they could phone him and reassure him, but he replied to say there was nothing they could do anyway, and that the chemotherapy had nearly killed him off last time, so he didn't want to go down that road again...he was giving up.

My friend Jane messaged to say she had been trying to email and thought my account had been hacked. That would make sense, as I still couldn't log on. But why would someone hack my email? The other alternative was that I had been locked out because of all the failed attempts. I gave her my password and asked her to investigate for me. Jane was as always so practical and got on with things.

I remembered hitching with another girlfriend called Jane in the back of a lorry when we were about 16 and ending up in London (all the way from Liverpool!), which was great! But then there was the issue of how on earth we were going to get back home, so we took our place on the side of the North Circular to hitch back. It was not such fun that time. We climbed up into a lorry's cab, and I ended up squashed in next to the driver, who kept putting his hand on my lap! Jane was safe next to the window. Thank God we were together...

I messaged Dr Thang and asked him to keep John positive (not virus positive, of course). I also said I wanted to be with John if he was dying. I couldn't imagine living without Juan, though, and couldn't stop crying. Thank goodness for his cap on my chest each night to comfort me. I now understood wanting to just touch the person you love when they are so ill.

Chris phoned me from Hoi Ann. I don't think he'd ever heard his mum crying before…not a good thing for me.

I had been in room 738 for five days, and in the hospital for 20 days. I hadn't seen John for nearly two weeks, and wondered if I would ever see him alive again. His body was already weakened from cancer; how would he survive this?

Jane messaged me to say she had got into my email with the help of her daughter. Thank goodness. At last I could pay some bills and catch up with everybody who had contacted me. I still hadn't heard anything about our backpack with the cash and credit cards, and John's luggage. To be honest, though, it just didn't seem that important.

Tuesday 27 March

There were still 153 confirmed cases, of which 111 were Vietnamese. The cases in Europe and the UK were in their thousands.

Almost immediately on waking I started crying again. I'd dreamt I was not with John and had kissed someone else. In fact it wasn't a dream, it was a nightmare, and it really upset me. Six days was too long to not see anyone apart from an odd glance, and not to be with John. I hadn't heard from Dr Thang, either. Had I upset him? Every time the door opened I jumped out of my skin. Was it bad news? Good news? This was a life-changing experience. Would I ever be the same fun-loving, adventurous person again? Would I stand up for myself more? Too many times I had let people take advantage of me, especially men, and I didn't want to lose the one man who loved me like an equal, and treated me like an equal, in every single way. I slipped over on the wet bathroom floor, and started crying again.

I phoned Sam as I knew this would make me feel happier. Strange that, asking your son for help, but then life is a circle and he listened and told me to be strong, as I always had been. He had no idea how strong I had been in my life. I had never told him or Chris about the men who had hurt me, the things that had happened to me – in between the good times – and I probably never would. There are some things you don't share with your children. Sam said the doctor had probably been really busy, and it wasn't personal or meant bad news.

Joe was also being a little more supportive, which really helped, and I prayed for a miracle. My friend Trudy, who had been on the same flight but down the back of the plane, prayed too – she had been moved to a room down the corridor – and I felt the strength from that.

Sam was right. Shortly afterwards Dr Thang messaged to say he had been really busy, and that John was still very ill but was a little bit stronger. He said his lungs were very badly damaged, but he was doing his best for him. I didn't doubt that for one minute.

After my unappetising lunch at 11.00am – we used to go out of the door like ants picking up our food – this time of soggy chips and cucumber and a slice of white bread. I guess they were trying to give me English food, but the sticky rice was better than the soggy chips! I phoned John, and had to hold back the tears. He sounded so weak and so confused.

Later on that evening John phoned me to say he was worried about our luggage, as he had still not received any of his. He sounded breathless and panicky, and I told him to stay calm and that I was trying to sort that. He then said he was being moved to the emergency ward and being put on a nebuliser, which I told him would be better for him. He asked me what my room number was, and I said 738, but he started getting confused again so we said goodbye.

At 8.53pm I got a message from Dr Thang – 'There is a problem.' This reminded me of, 'Houston, we have a problem', and I stared at the words. What did he mean? I messaged back, and my heart stopped when I saw the reply: John had been put on a ventilator. Oh God, no. Endotracheal intubation.

I was often told during my time on nights in operating theatres that nothing fazed me. I am a very calm person in stressful situations, who never panics, even when some pretty awful things were happening back then, like aortic aneurysms or road traffic accidents. What is the

Hilarious times with British Airways on 747 aircraft as a stewardess

Shan Meets The King!!

Flight VN 54 1st March 2020...
Culprit known as superspreader in the background

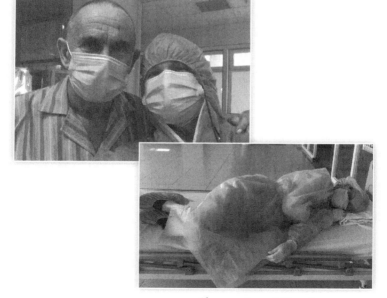

Shan arrives at Hanoi
The hospital for Tropical Diseases

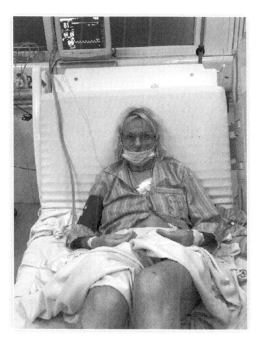

Not the best look, who cares - I was alive ... just!

The only ten minutes of fresh air I had in six weeks outside Hanoi Hospital with the press

Back to vibrant life again!

point of panicking, after all? It doesn't achieve anything. For some reason I recalled the night I was scrubbing up to assist in an operation, and my runner came in to tie up my green sterile gown at the back. The runner told me that Princess Diana had been involved in a car accident in Paris…and to this day I remember thinking *Here I am at the operating table, and at the same time Diana is being operated on to repair her damaged heart, quite literally.* I'd hoped they weren't panicking either.

But reading Dr Thang's reply, I was close to unravelling. I started writing in my notebook, frantically pouring my feelings onto paper before they got the better of me: *At least he is not struggling to breathe anymore… he will pull through…he has to…come on, Juan, your Boo-boo needs you…I am so sorry I brought you here…but you could have got it at home…and the care here is so much better…I can't live without my love…I just can't.*

I texted Joe, spoke to Sam, and texted Chris and my friend in Sydney. I also called Kathy at the embassy.

I asked Dr Thang if John could hear. Hearing is the last sense to go, and the first to come back. I said, "If he can hear me, I want to see him."

Wednesday 28 March

There were 169 cases, 21 recoveries, and no deaths in Vietnam. I hoped to God John wouldn't be the first death. In the UK there were thousands of cases and so many deaths.

I was not coping and woke up again after a nightmare that I couldn't recall this time. Groggily, I remembered I had drunk the miniature bottle of brandy I'd taken from the now-famous flight VN54. I hadn't been able to stick to having the 'one sip' I'd said I would have and had gulped the lot. I'd had no alcohol since the cocktails at the Metropole, when I'd drunk more than my fair share, so I think it had had even more of an effect.

There was no word about John's health. I was a mess. *Please do not die, John. I can't live without you. Please be OK.* I texted Richard and he told me he had asked the hospital's manager, Dr Giang, about me seeing John and, if possible, nursing him.

I started thinking of ways to see him, if I could sneak out in the night and grab the ID card for the lifts from the cupboard where I'd seen the nurses put it. But I was on the seventh floor, and John was now in ICU so perhaps that wasn't such a good plan. I even offered to be a nurse – I am a fully trained nurse, after all – and do bed baths, checking monitors, infusions, blood taking, anything…if just to get down to that floor and take care of John.

I kept thinking about the day I'd met John in my local church. I'd been in no mood for chatting, never mind anything else (I'd split from the boys' father a few months before), but I felt relaxed in his company and a couple of weeks later we decided to go for a walk at Goldhanger. John told me he loved me almost immediately, and said he'd like me to meet his two boys, and it wasn't that I didn't find him attractive – I did – but I was nowhere near ready for declarations like that or to meet his sons.

By November we were getting on so well, however, that we decided to have a few days away together. We stayed in Llanberis in Wales and woke up to a beautiful day. I said to John, "Let's climb Snowdon!" (I am inclined to announce such things without warning!) I informed the hotel staff and off we went, with loads of layers of clothes on. The last time I had climbed the mountain was when I had been training for the Grand Canyon. We soon got stuck into the climb. There was not a soul in sight, which was lovely, as in the summer the mountain is full of tourists.

It was sunny, but cold and very windy, but we were wrapped up well. It was that day that John said to me that due to his lungs being damaged by chemotherapy years before he could not climb hills…he hadn't mentioned mountains! I knew he could do it if we took it slowly, as by now we had walked for hours together when we met up. We were doing really well, and were about three-quarters of the way up, when I turned around to check on John – I had been walking slightly ahead. All I saw was John on the ground with blood all over his face.

I calmly walked down to him (with pace) thinking *Oh no, he's coughing up blood. I should not have taken him up Snowdon with his weak lungs,* and wondered what we would do so far from the hotel. When I reached him I was relieved to see that the blood was coming from his lip, and he explained that he had been blown over by a gust of wind and bitten it! In a second I went from being scared to now giggling hysterically as John asked if he'd got any teeth missing! In the next second a bearded man and his son appeared, who had travelled from Birmingham to climb the mountain, and they came over and offered a handkerchief to mop up the blood. They then offered us a gin and tonic out of his flask! "Have you got any lemon?" I asked, my scouse humour never far away. The next person who appeared was the ranger coming down the mountain, and he said not to go any further unless we had crampons and experience walking in the snow, so we had to turn back. We laughed all the way down and for the next two days.

Back to Hanoi Hilton… When my lunch arrived it was covered in peanuts. I'd already told them I was allergic to them. They tried so hard to please with the meals, but I was close to giving up.

After lunch I was spoken to by Dr Khiem, who was in charge of ICU. I asked to see John as I had been in isolation for nearly two weeks and had at least two negative swabs.

I enquired again about John's luggage and the backpack. A nurse with glasses finally said I would get everything on Monday as it had to be disinfected.

I Facetimed Chris. I felt bad because I had broken down on the phone to him. After all, John is not his father. But he was amazing, really supportive, and sent John a very loving text message…this meant so much to me.

By 10.00pm my Juan had been on the ventilator 24 hours, but I could hardly bear to think about that as it kept making me cry. I thought about lots of other things, random and sometimes silly things, just to pass the time, like having to sit in a circle on my very first day of school (I didn't want to go to school, not one bit), and having to sing 'Teddy Bears Picnic' – '*If you go down to the woods today, you're sure of a big surprise; If you go down to the woods today, you'd better go in disguise*' – which I thought was so babyish. And when I used to hold 'shows' in the garage and charge people a penny to come and watch. I would recite poems, one of them being 'The Spider and the Fly' by Mary Howitt, which was first published in 1829. '"*Will you walk into my parlour?" said the Spider to the Fly; "'Tis the prettiest little parlour that ever you did spy...*' My grandmother on my father's side helped me with this. We were very close, and many times, later on in my life, she would help me with my homework, especially French, which I hated. I'd also loved dressing up and was asked to be a flower girl at the local fete. I remembered seeing the flower queen and thinking how badly I'd wanted to be her! I'd spotted my lovely granny and father in the crowd and waved and waved. I was so proud and felt so special in my white frilly, netted dress with white spots on! I'd also taken part in the annual Lord Mayor's parade in Liverpool and was on one of the floats as a mermaid. (This had been, no doubt, the start of me wanting to enter all sorts of other contests.) I remembered being traumatised when my mum bit the head off the black jelly baby I had saved for when I'd finished the washing up. This was the end of the world as they were like little human beings to me!

A friend messaged me to say West Mersea was in complete lockdown, like the whole of the UK. But I couldn't think about anything other than being with John.

Thursday 29 March

There were now 188 cases in Vietnam and 25 recoveries. In the UK 209 had died.

I woke up feeling sick, but there was a message from Dr Khiem to say that John was stable. They had stopped sedation, and his ventilation had been dropped to 35%. *Oh thank goodness. Oh God, please let this miracle continue.* My mind was all over the place. I had been sleeping with John's cap on my chest, and Trudy had been praying for him all night. She had a spiritual side, like me, and I couldn't thank her enough.

We were supposed to be flying home today after an amazing holiday…but I looked around my prison-like cell, with its bars on the windows and my stripy jail pyjamas, and at the lovely clothes I'd bought with me, packed neatly in the suitcase, which I hadn't worn. It seemed like so long ago I'd packed them, excited about the trip and seeing Chris and all the sights.

I went to look out of the door down the corridor and was screamed at, as per usual: "Mask on! Go in your room!" I understood their fear, as they did not want this virus, but it was still awful. I had spotted that the room opposite was being fumigated by people who looked like something out of Star Wars films.

Dr Khiem asked me about John's lymphoma, and I

repeated what John had said about the hospital telling him there was nothing more they could do, but that it was dormant at the moment. But I asked Joe to contact Barts Hospital, and I emailed Professor Davies, who did John's six-month checks, to get his thoughts so I could update Dr Khiem. I asked him about seeing John, and he replied that it was "too difficult".

I stupidly opened the window again today because I was so desperate for some air, and was now battling flies and mosquitoes. I was also desperate for some company and had started having really odd thoughts. I needed to get out of that room before I went mad. It made me think about the school my parents sent me to, and feeling caged in and trapped and a bit claustrophobic. I was a Protestant for a start, and Upton was mostly run by Catholic nuns. One sister – Sister Albertine – I was terrified of. I did not fit in at all, but I did love the sports, especially long and high jump, and I was goalkeeper in hockey for the sixth form girls (I was only 13).

I remembered reading a magazine called *19* one day, loaned to me by one of the older girls from the hockey team. I had it hidden under the table and the nuns went mad, saying it was "filth". Later that day I saw a nun reading it… That made me furious. How come a 'holy' person could read it and I couldn't! A week later I saw a nun kissing another nun on a bench in the woods that we were forbidden to go to because men had been seen wandering about in there. I was so confused. A nun kissing another nun, and men in the woods – who were obviously bad people – so why were the nuns allowed in the woods? *'If you go down to the woods today, you're sure of a big surprise; If you go down to the woods today, you'd better go in disguise...'*

I thought about Sister Albertine years later when I married an Irish anaesthetist, who at one point was in a seminary to become a priest, and whose father was a Doctor who knew Sister Albertine. She would have had a fit if she'd known I was marrying into this large, close-knit family. Our wedding was only the second wedding ever to be held at the high altar at Liverpool Cathedral (Paddy's Wigwam, as it was so playfully called!), on 7 July 1979. The number seven has always featured in my life, and at times has felt like a lucky number for me. It was on the 7 July 2005 that I decided at the last minute not to take the Tube on that fatal day of the bombing of the Piccadilly line. And my entrance exam number for my state registered nurse exam had two number sevens in it.

Archbishop Derek Worlock officiated the marriage. When he was ill a few years later he asked me many times to visit him. But I had left Michael, and felt too ashamed, so I did not go. The marriage would never have worked as I was pressured into marrying him: Michael said he would commit suicide if I did not, and I can still see the bottom drawer in his small hospital bedroom with the drip ready to do the deed...

I thought about creating a virus advert: 'Care = Obedience and Vigilance; Ignore = Death', but when I ran it by Sam's girlfriend Jess she didn't think it was such a good idea.

By late afternoon there was no further news about

John and, although I hated to keep bothering the doctors, I messaged Dr Thang again.

Before the fated flight, we'd heard only 11 people had been sick with the virus in Vietnam. The newspapers had only just published an article about the 'super spreader' on our flight. It turned out she had not declared she had been to Italy, and I wondered what the rest of the media were saying about that. (Her sister was flown by private jet to Vietnam after she had arrived with us on our flight.) I thought about us sitting there on that plane, me reading the magazine that featured the fashion shows she had attended in Paris, Milan and London as an Instagram influencer, and John reading the newspaper that had first published the super spreader article, and once again could hardly believe how our holiday had turned into this.

Chris messaged me to say he had been ill with dengue fever, but had been ordered to a police station to be tested for Covid-19. Whatever next?

I was praying a great deal. Trudy was still praying too, in her room down the corridor. She told me she was a Sikh today. She was a very private person, so it surprised me that she told me this.

That night I looked at my hands whilst I was praying. My nails had got so long. I'd never had long nails in my life because of always working so hard. Funny I noticed that. And funny that I had a flashback just then – well, two actually – of my church in Stebbing, and on two occasions feeling very embarrassed. "Let us pray," our vicar had said one Sunday as the service got under way, and just at that quiet moment my phone rang full blast with Abba's song 'Dancing Queen' – the silence was over! I could have run out of the church there and then, but decided to stay for the prayer, with my face very red. I still love the song though! The other time I was really embarrassed was at one of the carol services. I was standing at the front of the church with the choir – I cannot sing at all, but love singing! – and halfway through I pressed the wrong button on my iPad and the words, "Siri is not available" blasted out, to the horror of the choir and congregation. I bet the choir were thinking it was a pity I was not available!

Thursday 30 March

My next nasal swab was negative. It seemed we needed four consecutive negative swabs before being discharged, and one had to be 24 hours before discharge. This information came from Detective Richard down the corridor.

Today for breakfast I was brought noodles and what looked like *giant* eyeballs, which just stared at me. (I was pretty sure they winked at me too!) I was so hungry I ate them. But I was also fascinated by what they might taste like. They tasted of nothing really, whatever they were, they were just a bit jelly-like.

It made me remember one lunchtime when I was doing my training in Jersey. I was having egg and chips in the canteen – the lovely girls on the till always undercharged me – and was happily tucking in when I noticed something a bit odd in amongst the chips. I looked a bit closer and noticed one of the nurses had hidden an amputated finger under my chips! The last time I had seen an amputated finger was one standing proud in a glass jar in a cabinet when I'd started my training. I screeched, much to the shock of the doctors on the doctors' table, and everyone else around me! And I was once sent to get a right fallopian tube by my nursing tutor, only to be told at the white line – the line that divides the theatre from the corridor – that they had run out… Gosh, I was gullible. If I'd known then I'd be working in theatres a few years' later.

I'd joined Colchester General's theatres with the NHS after leaving BA and I loved it. I was engaged and interested in what I was learning every single day. But their workload was truly huge, and they did (still do) such an amazing job despite the waiting lists and pressure. No day was ever the same. One day it would be general surgery, like bowel obstruction, another a fractured femur, and on Saturdays there would be far more emergency operations. There was no stopping me, and I went on to do an ENB 198 course for patients suffering from AIDS, a BTEC course on management, and an ENB 176 course for operating theatres.

There were so many memorable instances in the operating room…some of them unrepeatable! One I remember in particular. I was scrubbed up for a bowel obstruction and the patient became 'light' – in other words the anaesthetic was wearing off – and their left hand appeared from under the sterile sheets trying to get into their abdomen! I quickly alerted the anaesthetist...

I received a text from Joe to say that planes were the reason for the spreading virus. I didn't need to know that just at that moment, I just wanted some news about John. It was so awful not being able to be with him, to touch him and reassure him.

Still stuck in my room, I was still trying to drink at least one and a half litres of water a day, but I still had to sneak down the corridor when no one was looking.

Clean pyjamas and a clean sheet were still thrown through the door – great excitement! – and I had learnt to put a knot on each corner of the sheet, otherwise it slipped off the rubber mattress. I still did not have a pillow, so I continued to use a jacket I'd bought on eBay last year. And I still didn't have a towel either, so my pretty white cotton top was serving that purpose, kindly given to me by Sam's girlfriend Jess.

I was just getting changed into my clean pyjamas when there was a sharp knock on the door and a shout: "Put cothe on!" I had no idea what was happening, but suddenly there was a commotion outside in the corridor and the nurse said "Qwickwe!" so I grabbed the first pair of trousers I saw – a white pair – and a brightly coloured top. The trousers were hanging off me, so I had to hang on to them as I was pushed into a lift with some other patients and nurses. I still had no idea what was going on and, wow, suddenly I was shoved into bright, blinding daylight – and fresh air! – and saw camera crew and media people everywhere. I was confused. I had not been allowed to leave my room for nearly two weeks, or leave the hospital for nearly a month, and yet here I was surrounded by people and suddenly it was all OK?

Questions were being fired at us and, for some reason, they targeted me and started asking about John. It was too much, and I started crying, telling them he was in ICU.

One of the stewardess from our now-famous flight came up to me. She remembered me, and even which seat I had been in, and we hugged. She was so sweet and, gosh, I was so elated to breathe fresh air, see daylight, and touch someone that I could hardly speak. She said many of the flight crew had been ill, but because they'd worn masks at all times none of them had been really poorly. It was too late now, but why hadn't they asked us to wear masks? Perhaps they hadn't thought it was that bad, as until that point there were only those 11 cases in Vietnam and the masks were just a precaution. We'd had masks in our flight bags, but the virus was not being taken seriously in the UK.

And then it was all over and we were hurried back into the hospital and squashed back in the lift together. It didn't make sense, and I was lost for words. I wondered why Maisie had not been asked to come down, or Richard. But then I heard that Richard had done a Skype interview.

This short bit of film ended up on YouTube (this time with my boobs out of sight) and went viral. Over a third of the population of Vietnam viewed it, I was told.

I also appeared on the news with pictures of John

before he was put on the ventilator, and hundreds of heartfelt comments were made.

My phone rang then and it was a woman, sounding hysterical. I didn't know who it was but she kept screaming, "Tony's dead! Tony's dead!" At first I was sure I didn't know a Tony, and then I remembered our neighbour over the road. I realised after asking the woman to please speak slowly that it was our other neighbour, dear Percephine, who confirmed that, yes, Tony was dead. I was so shocked. I had been texting his wife Rosie just a couple of days before, and had advised her to tell Tony to get tested as it seemed he had the symptoms. They had taken him to hospital, but five minutes later he had collapsed. Tony was younger than us, and a fit man, and I could hardly believe it.

I started crying again. Why had I booked this trip? I'd wanted to see my son, but John hadn't needed to come. He'd said he was concerned about his weak lungs and that if he caught the virus it would "be the end" for him; but he'd also heard there were only 11 cases in Vietnam, and he'd always wanted to see this part of the world, so I'd booked tickets on that plane for us both. The plane with the super spreader onboard. But John could have got the virus at home anyway…my emotions were in turmoil.

I received a text from Dr Khiem suggesting that I could do a video call to John. I had been trying to convince him that if John saw me it would help his recovery, and a video call would have to do for now. But I needed help. I'm not that good with technology, and scuttled down the corridor near Richard's room so he could help me set it up – the nurses didn't stop me. I guessed that after being rushed outside for an interview with tonnes of other people they couldn't force me to stay in my room anymore.

After some fiddling the video call to John was connected and, oh my goodness, I could not believe what he looked like. His face was like a massive dark-coloured balloon with tubes coming out of it, and all of his hair had gone. All of his beautiful curls, all disappeared. Oh, my darling John. Richard went as white as a sheet when he saw him, and was visibly upset. They had built up quite a rapport when they'd been in the same room together, praying for me to get well, and he too could hardly believe what he was seeing. Was it the shock of the virus to his body? I keep a lock of my mother's hair under my pillow at home, as a comfort; but I would have no such thing if John died. Where had they put his hair? It would have been swept up by the cleaner in her yellow wellies. I was so upset, but I waved a Snickers bar in front of my phone – his favourite – that I'd kept for him as a treat, and babbled on about how much I loved him, hoping he would be able to see and hear me, and the Snickers bar.

I have only ever looked at a recording of this video once, and have never shown it to anyone. It was one of the most distressing moments of my entire life and I have no wish to relive it.

Friday 31 March

There were 203 cases in Vietnam, 55 recovered, and no deaths.

I had a message to say they were going to try and get John off the ventilator. I was so happy. Maisie's husband was still on his, but he was not as fit as John, and she was still so worried. Thank God for our long walks in Portugal and Wales and a good diet.

I remember saying to Dr Khiem, "Please don't let him die. I know he's 73 but he's a fit man," and he assured me he would not let him die…a very brave and bold thing to say, but a lovely thing to hear.

Shortly afterwards a nurse came to tell me I could see John if I wore full PPE gear, and I went to tell Maisie. She told me she already knew. I was stunned. How unkind to not tell me when Trudy and I had been praying for John and her husband, and I'd been the one pushing to see them, and persuading the doctors that it would help their recovery. Why had she done that? (She later admitted she had been hanging onto my coat tails, due to my experience as a nurse, in helping us get into ICU.)

Anyway, I was very excited and wondered if my interview with the press had helped, as I had praised the hospital and the staff for their amazing care. (Dr Giang, the big boss, had always said to me that not even he was allowed in ICU.) The Vietnamese are very proud people, and I believe the government own most of the TV channels, so good PR never goes amiss… The short story was, I had probably helped them, so they were helping me.

It was now John's fourth day on a ventilator, and 17 days since I'd seen him, so I stopped thinking about why it was I had been allowed out only just now. I didn't care right then, I just cared about seeing him.

Maisie and I were dressed in full PPE and, with security everywhere, were escorted to the lift and down to ICU. We were then asked to take that PPE off and put another lot on, and shown the 'clean' and 'dirty' areas to change in. I hadn't been down to this floor for weeks and noticed the huge Perspex screen across the nurses' station, the isolation tents, and dozens more ventilators...

My mask started steaming up with the tears streaming down my face when we were taken into ICU, and I started shaking and sat down next to John, who was in a full oxygen mask, and started speaking to him. And then I heard a nurse's sweet voice: "Missa Dixong ower here." I looked closer at the man I had been talking to, and it was not John, so I looked at where she was pointing, and there he was. I went over to him and sat down, shaking so much. John had a full oxygen mask on too, and could not speak, but he managed to raise his hand and blow me a kiss. I barely recognised him. *Oh, John.* My heart was pounding so irregularly I thought I might have a heart attack. My tears were still falling, and then I realised his hair hadn't fallen out, he had been shaved as a precaution, like they used to back in the seventies when I was training as a nurse. Vietnam was still old-school, of course, and they had done what used to be done to prevent cross-contamination in theatres. What an amazing job they had done taking care of my beloved. (But thank goodness they hadn't shaved me!)

It was then I realised that John might just make it, and was overwhelmed with gratitude for everyone's prayers. Even Rosie, our neighbour, had texted me, despite her husband dying only yesterday from the virus.

Maisie left before me, saying that her husband wasn't making any sense and was really confused. She also said it had exhausted her coming down here, and it was then that I remembered how ill I had been just two weeks ago, but how I was now able to walk about and shower. I sat with John a long time, holding his hand and squeezing his arm, but finally said goodbye, not sure when I would be allowed to see him again. I told him I loved him and to get well and I'd see him soon. I was tired, but so happy. I just knew John would be OK now, and for the first time I imagined us getting out of here, getting home, doing normal things again...

I put the TV on back in my room and saw that Prince Charles was out of isolation a week after his diagnosis. Why were the UK not understanding how serious this was, despite having so many deaths?!

I could feel myself changing, getting braver, getting more confident in my thoughts. I would speak my mind about this, and I would do it in front of the cameras. I had always loved the limelight as a little girl – what had happened to that little girl, and the young woman who won Miss Jersey and paraded on floats and did interviews? – and I would do it again, and I would not be afraid.

Saturday 1 April

Vietnam had 212 cases, 58 recoveries, and no deaths. A total of 563 had died in one day in the UK.

We had been in hospital for 26 days.

I slept well but awoke feeling a bit light-headed and dizzy. I was worried, and hoped I would not succumb to the virus again. I had been told it might be possible even though I was so much better.

John's luggage and the backpack finally arrived today, but I was unable to see him.

Joe called me about our insurance documents and I asked him to contact Professor Davies himself as I'd still not heard from him about management of John's lymphoma.

I took some glucose today, suggested by Trudy, and it helped a great deal with my energy as I was still feeling light-headed and dizzy.

Sunday 2 April

I was allowed to see John today – and he was very confused. He did not know he was in Vietnam. He thought he was in Canada, I guess because he could see trees out of a distant window. He had a much better view than mine, but I think he deserved it and needed it.

He then asked me, "Are you enjoying Daffodil Hotel?", which tickled me pink! Where had that come from? Then he said, "Right, let's go! I'm better! We'd better book a flight!" Gosh…what drugs was he on? LSD or something? The man could not walk, had a catheter in, ECG leads, two intravenous infusions and an oxygen mask! Then he said he wanted a pink bag for his rubbish…and that's when I realised that, despite being confused, he was definitely improving, because we have an in-house joke about him going to the rubbish tip all the time at home with his pink plastic bin bags! They must be missing him!

I got Dr Khiem to contact Barts after he told me that there were many nodules on John's lung. These were probably there before, and when I spoke to John he said they weren't Lily reappearing, and I was relieved to hear him talking that way. When I left the ITU girls were taking photos of me. I was famous since my TV interview!

I was on a high when I got back to my room, and popped in to Maisie to reassure her that her husband's confusion was normal. She didn't look that interested and was typing into her laptop. And then a nurse came in and told me I was being moved…into Maisie's room! My happy bubble from seeing John burst in a split second. Maisie went ballistic (which is putting it mildly) and started shouting, "No! This is NOT GOING TO HAPPEN! I am going to be here a long time and I NEED MY OWN ROOM!"

I went into my calm mode and quietly told her that there were other patients in the hospital who needed the beds up here, not just her, but in all truth I was horrified. This woman obviously disliked me more than she had previously let on, plus I was very embarrassed about her behaviour. I don't know what this display of temper was telling them about Maisie, but it can't have been good. The nurse said to me that I needed to get my stuff and move now, but Maisie was still shouting, "NO! NO!"

I needed John's happy drugs.

I went back to my room and texted Richard. Ever resourceful, he did a drive-by past her room and saw that she was moving the furniture around to make her space in the room as large as possible, and mine as small as possible. Funny how she found the energy to do that... He also noted that she did not have a fridge, and we quickly moved the fridge from my room into Maisie's. He told me he had beer in his fridge (the Germans in his room had somehow got it into the hospital), which, despite the horrible circumstances, made me laugh. Richard was then told to leave, so I had to push my bed into Maisie's room on my own, which was exhausting as I was hardly back to full strength. The nurses did not help, as they were still so fearful of the virus, and did not even hold the door open, so I bashed the bed into the wall, chipping off a large chunk of plaster, and banged the door. (I bet the damage is still there on that wall in her room! I had left my mark!)

When the bed was in place I pushed the bedside cabinet alongside it, near my head, so at least I would not see Maisie all the time and she could have her privacy. You could hear a pin drop. How could this be happening? How could I be sharing a room with the most unfriendly, angry woman I had ever met?

Richard texted me to see how I was. He was getting agitated now and had been in touch with Kathy from the embassy. The Germans in his room had had four negative swabs, as had he, and he wanted to leave. They had flights booked for tomorrow, so why couldn't he book a flight? Why had the German embassy been so efficient and the British embassy so useless? Kathy seemed to be scared of the doctors and unwilling to talk to them to arrange anything for him.

I only needed one more negative swab, but I wouldn't be leaving without John. And if they sent me to quarantine in a hotel, they wouldn't let me back in to see him, so I needed to stay where I was. I sent a strong email to Kathy telling her that I did not want any holdups when we left. My clothes in my suitcase had hardly been moved, and neither had John's, so we were ready to go home just as soon as he was strong enough. Suddenly all I wanted was to get home.

I asked Dr Thang to send my hospital notes to my insurance company, but I don't think he understood, so I then asked him to at least give me some paperwork that showed I'd had the virus and was now negative.

I opened my fridge and was astonished to see two beers! Richard must have put them in there! Hmmm...a dilemma. Should I offer one to Maisie or not? My feeling was, *No way*! But I did in the end, and she refused – phew! It was the first alcoholic drink I'd had since I'd gulped the brandy I brought with me from the plane.

Trudy's next test came up as positive, after four negative ones, yet she was told she wouldn't be going back to the UK and was distraught. She had been asymptomatic the whole time she had been at the hospital. I tried to help her as she had me, and said to try and pretend she was on a retreat, but she really was very upset.

Monday 3 April

Cases in Vietnam 233, and no deaths. Over 3,000 deaths in the UK.

I contacted Trail Finders, who said they would sort our flights out when we were ready to leave. I didn't trust Kathy to do anything, but had every confidence in them. The food hampers had been such a blessing, and we had been so grateful, but they had stopped now the country was in complete lockdown. I did speak to Kathy though, and I was quite abrupt with her, saying, "Please make sure all our paperwork is ready as we want absolutely no holdups your end." I found out from Google that Kathy had the same surname as the consular general. She probably got the job because of her connection to him. She sounded lovely, but was completely out of her depth.

Tuesday 4 April

This morning a Dr Young asked me to fill in a research form and I said yes. (He was a student doctor, I think.) The doctors had taken such good care of us, so I would do anything to help them.

I went to see John again and was amazed. There was so much improvement! He told me he loved me, and thanked me for coming into his life. He said he felt positive at last, and kept asking about a flight home, but he had no idea about the masses of paperwork that needed to be filled in, plus he still could not walk – he couldn't even get out of bed. I explained that he needed to be as fit as possible before we travelled and, without going into too much detail, told him that things were quite bad in the UK so we had to be absolutely sure we were both as strong as possible before we went back. But, gosh, it was so good to hear him talking and he looked so much better that I took a photograph of him for Joe. It was hard to look at the other photo, the 'before' photo, but the difference to the 'after' photo was amazing.

Dr Khiem messaged me to say he had spoken to Professor Davies in Barts hospital in London, who said no treatment was needed for John's previous lymphoma.

Maisie and I were sort of getting along OK, particularly after I scrubbed her bathroom and cleared out the drain – as I was now quite the expert. (I think she felt such a task was beneath her). She was amazed at how the water now disappeared and said it was disgusting that the cleaners did not do this job. I said they were obviously still petrified of coming near us, as were the nurses, as they still left our food outside the room. I'd decided that if I was going to share a room with her I did not want any issues or arguments, and always asked Maisie if she wanted to shower first. Anything for a quiet life.

Sam texted me to say Jess was pressure washing the

patio at our home in West Mersea, and he was weeding and sanding down his boat, *Barracai,* ready for the fishing season. Sam always was, and still is, such a kind person. I'll never forget the Christmas Day Sam wanted to give all his presents from Father Christmas to other children, and he wanted him to deliver them. But he'll never forget the Christmas Day I gave him a couple of second-hand action men…who had toothmarks in their legs. I said it was because they had "been in action"! (Those were the days when money was very scarce.)

Chris messaged to say he was hiking in a nature reserve and sent me a picture of a thousand-year-old tree. And Jane sent some funny videos from Wales. All of these things lifted my spirits. They felt 'normal'. It was lovely to receive those texts and messages and enjoy all the funny memories.

Wednesday 5 April

I sent a 'round robin' text out to the friends I'd made in the hospital – and another big thank you to Richard for showing me how to do this too! – and we met up at 7.00pm at the corner of the corridor with a glass of water in hand, pretending it was a sherry, as we had done a few times before! The nurses always went for a break then, so we could speak and have a giggle without being shooed back into our rooms.

I went to look out of the window and saw the nurses doing yoga in the courtyard, and oh how I wished I could join them. Seeing them reminded me to do some more sit-ups. I then went back to the corridor and chatted with an American guy who lives in Vietnam, and who was sharing the same room as Richard, who was also desperate to get out.

Thursday 6 April

I found out online – I didn't dare put the TV on in our room as Maisie didn't like it; although to be honest I was still sensitive to the noise (I still am now), and didn't mind that much – that Boris Johnson was in ICU with the virus, but not ventilated. I also watched the Queen make a speech to the UK, which was quite moving and made me feel like we were in a war…which we sort of were.

There was a bang on the door and a nurse shouted, "Now! To ICU!" I really needed the loo, and Maisie was in a dither, but there was no time to think, never mind pee, as we were taken down in the lift and put into PPE gear. I was stunned to see a TV camera crew there, pointing their cameras and microphones at John.

They started speaking to me and filming, asking about John and me, and I told them how wonderful the doctors had been, and that safety was very important here in Vietnam, which was why there had been no deaths. I was braver now and said that there must be a reason why England was having so many deaths, and that Vietnam had done a great job in my eyes, and was a country that had handled the virus perfectly. John perked up no end after the TV interview!

When I went back up to my floor Trudy was very angry about Kathy at the embassy, but Maisie started praising Kathy, saying she thought she was wonderful. Perhaps she liked the thought that she was communicating directly with someone from the embassy. This made me smile. I hadn't told her I'd dated a consul – a consulate diplomat, in fact – when I was just 17. He had been 12 years older than me, and I had got used to being driven around in his official car with the 'CD' badge on, drinking champagne with him in beautiful places, and generally enjoying the high life.

I'd only started seeing the consulate because of breaking up with one of his friends, Jorge Gonzalez, whose father was a Venezuelan diplomat. I'm not sure what Jorge did. Not much I don't think. Anyway, he was handsome, and we had fun together.

One night we'd been to the Moby Dick in the Wirral, and met up with my chums Tommo, Cottie, Rog, Sid and Ibbo. Dante, Jorge's friend, offered us a lift home. Their other friend Miguel got in the front, and Jorge and I got in the back, and were heading down Column Road in West Kirby when a tyre burst. The car overturned, and the next thing I remembered was being in an ambulance and shouting, "Get me to the hospital!" and the doctors asking for my name and address. I was petrified of what my father would say if he found out where I'd been (I was supposed to be at a friend's house), so I refused to tell them.

I only remember part of my time in hospital. I was put on diamorphine (heroin) for pain – I was black and blue all over, and also had severe internal bleeding and a damaged right kidney (which I nearly lost) – and remember saying to the nurse who was doing my blood pressure to look, please, and not take my blood pressure because it was making my arm black, which of course it wasn't…the bruising was from the car crash. I used to watch the clock hands move minute by minute, waiting for my next injection. Heroin is a highly addictive drug, and it hadn't taken long for me to want the next hit.

It was an awful shock for my parents when the police knocked on their front door at 11.00pm to say I had been involved in a car accident. Someone must have given them my address. Mum brought champagne in to celebrate I was alive, and for once I refused it. But she insisted and I vomited straightaway. What a waste. I'd ended the relationship with Jorge shortly afterwards because I was told the flowers he had brought me he had stolen from a graveyard. I was not amused. Enter Dante, who within weeks had asked me to marry him. I was not even 18 years old! When I told my father he said, "When you have a qualification you can get married." Thank God for his strong character. It was why I'd stuck at nursing.

I'd recently met up with a girl called Alex whilst walking in Wales. We'd started chatting, like people sometimes do on walks, and it turned out she'd been walking on the side of the road that night of the car crash and was the one who'd called the ambulance. I had no memory of this. She said she had been so worried because my abdomen was so swollen. How lovely, and amazing, to meet her after so many years, and how lucky it was that we all survived that night.

I thought about that accident, and surviving, and I wondered whether Maisie would have treated me differently if she knew anything about me. I doubted it.

Friday 7 April

245 cases now in Vietnam.

I went down to ICU again and Dr Khiem wanted to talk to me. John was feeling low because he could not pass urine. He'd had his catheter removed, but it'd had to be reinserted and he was in a lot of pain. Dr Khiem also said John had an enlarged prostate. A healthy prostate should weigh about 30 grams, but John's was at least 90 grams, and he was worried about cancer again. My heart sank. Oh no, not another issue to deal with... But I knew we had to make one step at a time. Besides, I remembered that an enlarged prostate is almost always benign. We needed to get John moving, to get his blood moving, but I was worried he was still too weak. Just before I left John again asked me how Daffodil Hotel was. Wherever it was in his head, he seemed happy about the place. It sounded lovely!

I noticed as I left, for the first time, that the patient in the opposite cubicle to John was also shaved. I looked closer and realised it was the culprit's aunt, the woman who'd had the antiviral HIV drug and who had brought the bag of apples in. She was still looking extremely ill, after all this time. I asked about her, and was told she'd had a slight bleed on the brain. Once again, no patient confidentiality in Vietnam.

Doctor Phuc, who seemed to run ICU with Dr Khiem, said John needed a trans urethral resection of the prostate, and that they would try and get it done at the hospital as soon as John had a negative swab. I couldn't believe it. You would wait months for this op in the UK, and here in Vietnam it seemed it could be done almost immediately.

I was told that Vietnam News wanted to interview me again for TV, as they liked my video.

Saturday 8 April

I received a phone call to say the crew wanted me to do an interview now. Wow, these people from national TV really liked to give you a warning they were coming. I was still in my stripy pyjamas, with wet hair from the shower and no makeup on. The room was so noisy too, as they were fumigating next door. I hustled Maisie out of the door. It would just be a distraction her being there.

The interview lasted 34 minutes, and I propped my phone up on my bedside cabinet against a dirty old razor and the pot of face cream I had purchased at the pearl shop on the way to Halong Bay, and recorded it. I said at the end of the interview that if there was a positive to come out of all this, it should be to be kind, and realise the important people in this world were doctors, nurses and cleaners, not celebrities.

After the interview I went down to ICU to see John, and went through the whole performance of PPE, which I knew was necessary. I think Dr Khiem realised I didn't need escorting each time as I knew all the gowning-up rules and how to dispose of them, so he pointed to the emergency stairs and indicated that I could use those rather than be escorted in the lift every time. What a star! And it felt like I was making a great escape! If he'd spoken more English, I would have told him about escaping the matron when I was in bed in the doctors' quarters! I had to clamber over four balconies to get away from her! I didn't get away with it, of course, and the next day I was summoned to matron's office. They'd had a call from the *News of the World* to say that a doctor had not answered his bleep for a cardiac arrest as he was in bed with Miss Jersey (it was just after I'd won the competition). It turned out that my jealous ex had called the paper hoping that the doctor would get the sack and leave the island (but as it was not true, this did not happen). It was the same matron who, when she heard I had entered the Miss Jersey competition, called me to her office. I thought she was going to congratulate me, but she said, "I train nurses, not beauty queens! You must not continue with this contest!" And when I told her I had...erm...won, she nearly fell off her chair a second time! (The first time was when she interviewed me and I was wearing a black mini dress that barely covered my bottom and white leather boots!) She was so scary, but had such a good soul.

She reminded me of the actress Hattie Jacques.

Whilst no one was looking I nipped down the stairs – what fun! – and gowned-up and went into ICU. The nurses and doctors smiled at me, and I noticed the TV crew were filming the very poorly aunt, and then they turned their camera on us.

I started to get John to move his legs up and down, ready to start walking again. There seemed to be no physio available, despite the medical care being fantastic. Our priority now was to get him a negative test so we could get the prostatectomy operation done, and to get him strong enough for the op and our flight home.

Trudy, my lovely Indian spiritual friend, told me she would be finally leaving tomorrow. She had been very supportive when John had been so ill, and we'd texted each other a lot, and prayed. I was so happy for her but I knew I'd miss our chats outside her door, when I used to sneak out of my room to meet her.

Sunday 9 April

There were 251 cases in Vietnam, 126 recovering and still no deaths. The cases in the UK were still in the thousands.

I woke up feeling low but, hey, I was no longer white as a sheet. My hair had started falling out though, in handfuls, which was horrible, and I was really glad my HRT had been replaced again. The hair loss made me think that at least I had not been shaved like John or the culprits aunt. A girl across the corridor called Ellen, who spoke good English, managed to get the HRT for me and I was really grateful. It was twice the dosage of my regular HRT, so I decided to just take one tablet every other day and hoped it wouldn't trigger any bleeding.

Dr Khiem said it would be too difficult for John to get his op done in Vietnam due to politics and other stuff, which was disappointing but I understood. He then asked me to be present when he tried to get John to pass urine after removal of the second catheter. I said I would run the tap, but he was not having any of that and wanted me for moral support only. Success! John peed! The other good news was that John managed to stand on his own! He also asked for his phone so he could wish everyone a happy Easter (Easter was earlier in Vietnam than in the UK), which was great as he was obviously feeling strong enough to do that. It made me love him so much.

Sam messaged me to say all the weeding and pressure washing of the patio was done at our home, which was great, and his fishing boat looked remarkably good. He'd also had two lobster pots made by hand by a lovely lady, so I was looking forward to munching on one of those juicy lobsters – bliss compared to prawns the size of grubs (and just as gristly) once a week. I was lucky because Maisie gave me hers as she did not like them; but I reckoned she had a secret supply of food somewhere as she hardly ate anything we were given.

I Facetimed Chris but there was no reply. I hoped he was OK.

Maisie and I actually watched a film on her laptop that evening. She still wouldn't put the TV on, but it didn't bother me. The film was rather sad, but it passed the time. I still have no idea to this day what it was!

Monday 10 April

I spoke to Sam and he said he'd been fishing, which made me laugh. I remember when he was a little boy he used to go fishing with his brother and used to moan that it was "the most boring thing on earth!" I love boats and sailing (I still do, and am happiest on the water), and remembered the time my father was building a trimaran and I helped him to fibreglass it. Dad had this dream of sailing it around the world. I do not remember ever sailing on her, but I do remember the gale-force winds one weekend and many boats being wrecked. Dad's trimaran suffered a hole in the main hull, which he showed me, and was quite proud that it did not sink, explaining that this was why it was a safer boat to sail than a single hull. Dad gave the boat away in the end, and I found it years later in Porthmadog boat yard. I hoped the owner had more luck than my father and got to sail her. Dad and I had some fun fibre glassing her together, though.

I knew I was being swabbed that morning and so hoped it would be negative. I did some running up and down the stairs to work on my fitness and make my lungs stronger – and see John, of course, who was sitting up. He even went for a very slow, short, wobbly walk, and we had our first kiss in weeks, albeit through masks! The TV crew were there again and filmed us…hmmm…I never thought I'd get fed up with being filmed, but this time it felt quite intrusive. They filmed me through the window of my room too, while I was eating, and I started to feel a bit paparazzied.

Maisie wasn't doing too well. She wasn't as athletic as me in the first place, or as keen to stay fit as best she could whilst in hospital. We're all different, I guess. She did not spend as much time in ICU as I did, as she felt too exhausted afterwards, and yet she was still asymptomatic.

Tuesday 11 April

In Vietnam there were 257 cases, 144 recoveries and no deaths. There were still thousands of cases in the UK.

TV Vietnam and Talk Vietnam burst into our room this morning as I was coming out of the shower. Maisie was not happy, as you can imagine, and neither was I, and I told them to come back in half an hour. They seemed to think they owned us.

I phoned a woman called Leigh from the TV station, as we'd become friends, and she was very apologetic. (She would also help a great deal later on.) I then spoke to Huyen (from the TV station), who said she would send me the link to the last filming they did. She told me they wanted to do two episodes, one with a French ambassador who was married to a Vietnamese girl, and the other with me, but they needed to film again as the sound wasn't very good the first time.

I was swabbed again by the doctor who only said

three words: "'Ore froat? 'Edake?"

I went down to see John again, striding down the stairs with Maisie lagging behind. John had a catheter back in as he was not peeing again. I showed him the picture on my phone of me jumping off the cliff into a massive waterfall in the Grand Canyon...no peeing. I then showed him a video I had of Victoria Falls, but still no peeing. Not a good sign if not even Victoria Falls does the trick. We decided to have another go tomorrow because John was getting quite distressed.

I phoned my dear godfather (and friend) Fabby, a retired consultant, to see if he could organise a prostatectomy for John. He said no non-emergency operations were being done in the UK.

The TV crews didn't come back so I guessed they would be coming another day.

Wednesday 12 April

Vietnam had 260 cases, no deaths. Usual high deaths in the UK.

Dr Khiem texted me to say John's catheter was out again and could I come down, so I went to see John on my own, without Maisie dragging along behind. He was feeling down and so wanted to be able to pee. After seven attempts he peed like Niagara, and it happened so fast we couldn't get a sample! Oh well, we'd have to wait for the next time.

John had saved me a chocolate bar – oh, wow, what

a man – that the nurses had given him, because they adored him and gave it to him as a treat. It had peanuts in, however, so that was that.

The culprit's aunt was now off her ventilator but had had a tracheostomy. Thank goodness John had avoided that. I still wondered how the culprit of seat 5k felt about having infected so many people. I'd heard that her two chauffeurs were infected too, and one was on oxygen and one was in ICU.

The TV people phoned. They wanted to interview me again tomorrow at 11.00am, with a doctor, and talk about my bleeding. My bleeding? I wasn't bleeding. I must have mentioned to someone that HRT can cause bleeding. I said I was sad that she knew this, and she apologised. But that was a no from me.

Kathy from the embassy phoned and said she was sorting everything out. Right…

I texted Joe to say we were working on getting John stronger before we made the trip home. The doctors said he needed at least another week. But at 3.00pm there was a newsflash from the embassy on Maisie's laptop that said the last direct flight would be leaving tonight, and there would not be another one for at least another month, if not more. (Strange that Kathy made no mention of this when she called…)

I just knew I had to get John on this last direct flight…he would not survive going via Doha, a 36-hour flight which the others had done, including detective and resourceful friend Richard.

Wednesday 12 April cont.

Writing this bit, the film *Carry on Nursing* comes to mind! I ran out of the room to get to ITU, but the double doors that were normally open were padlocked! I somehow managed to pull the padlock chain over the bar and opened the doors and hurtled down the back stairs – like a relative of mine, Herbert Drury, who won a bronze medal in the 1912 Olympics for gymnastics! Whilst no one was looking, I put my PPE on in the corridor and threw myself into ICU.

The doctors and nurses were stunned to see me as they had been watching the monitors, including John's, and I explained that I wanted to get John out of there, that night, all translated via Google on my phone. They all looked shocked. They'd had no deaths, and certainly did not want one now, but I asked again if there was any way this was possible. There was a deadly silence. Had they understood me?

My mind was buzzing. Was I mad? I needed all our discharge paperwork from the Ministry of Health, needed to pay our hospital bills and get valid receipts for our insurance companies, get proof of our four negative swabs, get our medical notes for our insurance companies, and book the flights, plus get the efficient Kathy to do everything that needed doing her end. I looked at John. He was slumped in his bed as if he had had a stroke. He still looked so ill. Could we do this? Should we?

I spoke to John and told him about the flight. He looked sort of excited, but was worried he would not be able to pass urine on the flight – and quite rightly so, as we did not want him going into retention on board.

I went back and spoke to the doctors and they agreed that if I could give him injections during the flight to stop thrombosis, and John was happy to have a catheter fitted again for the flight, then it was possible. I missed nursing and was more than happy to take on that role again if it meant I could get John home. I agreed to monitor him and administer the injections, and John agreed to be catheterised.

I disappeared back to my floor. There was loads to do. I had no idea when the flight would be leaving – Kathy could sort that out – I just knew that it left tonight and we needed to be on it.

I banged on the glass window of the nurses' station and they just stared at me. None of them spoke English. Eventually I managed to beckon one of them enough to come out, but it didn't help much because she still didn't understand what I was saying, despite Google, so I started looking through all the windows to see if I could find someone who could translate. Thankfully a Vietnamese lady appeared who spoke English with an American accent and she explained that I needed our discharge paperwork – which Richard had told me took 48 hours to organise – and proof of my four negative swabs. I knew ICU would prove John's and organise his discharge, but I needed to produce evidence of mine. After a lot of discussion about my paperwork I was handed a bill for my food…

In disbelief I looked at the bill in my hand. The

total was in Vietnamese dongs, and I didn't have a clue how much it was and I honestly didn't care. I tried to explain to the nurse (the Vietnamese/American lady had gone) that I only had US dollars. What followed was a ridiculous case of me having to go up and down seven flights of stairs three times to get to the ground-floor pharmacy, where I was told to take the bill to pay it, and back to sort this out.

The ground floor was another world to me after all this time, but I found the pharmacy and tried to pay the bill with my US dollars, which they would not accept. I went back up for my bank cards, but none of them would work for some reason – most likely a problem with their card machine. I again handed them a bunch of US notes, but they shook their heads, so back upstairs I went to try and communicate with the nurses again. Eventually they wrote the bill out in US dollars, which was only $55 to be exact, and back down I went to the pharmacy. I handed the nurse $60 and said I did not want the change – I was so tired and so frustrated by then and had started crying, so I just walked away – but up she came to the seventh floor to bring me my $5 change. I felt bad then for getting upset, and I wondered if they'd think I was weak...I still needed to get my discharge papers from them!

Next I needed to sort out our other papers for travelling, so I phoned Kathy to tell her we were leaving on the last direct flight to the UK that night. "Yes, I suppose you could do that..." she said. I couldn't believe it. *Yes, I suppose you could do that...* And then she said I'd have to book the flights through our travel agent, but she would make sure we were not charged for overstaying our one-month visa. Well done, Kathy... I realised I was not going to get anywhere with her and ended the call. I phoned Trail Finders and they told me to contact London Trail Finders, but when I called them they said the flights would have to be booked in Vietnam... After another call to Trail Finders, who I thought would be so helpful, I gave up. I'd book the flights myself.

I went onto the Vietnamese Airlines website and all was going quite well until I came to pay and it said the session had expired. I repeated this exercise twice, to no avail. By now it was 9.30pm at night and I'd found out that the flight was at midnight. I still had no discharge paperwork, I hadn't heard back from Kathy, I hadn't booked any transport to the airport, and I still needed the proof of four negative swabs... Would all this ever get done?

Maisie was in shock that we were leaving with so little time to organise anything, and I was starting to think *Can I really do this*? I knocked on the door of the window of the nurses' station on my floor and, at last, they gave me my discharge letters, so I phoned Joe and told him we were flying back tonight. He started saying that John's insurance would be nullified if I gave him injections on the plane to stop thrombosis. What? That surely wasn't the case, and I was already stressed so I ended the call. If the doctors had said it was OK, then I trusted them. I then phoned Sam and told him we were hoping to be at Heathrow in the morning. He said he would be there. (He did admit a few weeks later that he thought I had finally lost the plot, but also knew he would be there at Heathrow whether we arrived or not.)

It was now 10.00pm and I needed to get down to John and give him some clothes to put on, but I still hadn't had an email confirming the flights I had booked. I really was panicking now, which was not like me, and couldn't believe it when I saw the TV crews, loads of them, filming outside the ICU. I was trying to get into my PPE gear and get into ICU and said, "Please, no filming!" as I frantically checked my phone again for an email. I had no internet service! I was in a state by now, but spotted Leigh, the lovely lady presenter of the TV channel. I explained what was happening and she was brilliant and asked if she could use the ICU computer. They said yes and she managed to book two flights. I had no clue how much they were. They were millions of dongs. I did not care. I just wanted to get us on that flight. (It turned out I had booked and paid for four flights…!)

I started to get John dressed, but he seemed forlorn with his catheter in and cardiac leads attached, and then I was called in to see the doctors. Dr Khiem was there, and Dr Phuc. They were all there. I looked at their faces and my heart nearly stopped when they said, "There is a problem." "What is it?" I asked calmly, but inside there was a raging pain in my chest. They told me John had a very high temperature and they did not know why. I couldn't believe it. I knew John could not fly with a temperature. And I didn't want him to. How could I live with myself if he died on the flight? "Is there anything we can do?" I asked.

After a lot of discussion they agreed that if I gave John all the other medication he now needed on the flight, they would discharge him, which I told them I would. The flight was leaving in an hour and a half.

I rushed to get John dressed with the help of a wonderful nurse, who had obviously grown very attached to him. The travel agency must have arranged our taxi driver, as Vinnie was waiting for us outside. The TV crew started filming as we left, with the consultants and doctors carrying our suitcases, and the nurse's little face at the ICU window as she waved goodbye. (I was very nearly in tears writing this.) I cannot tell you how emotional it was saying goodbye to our 'home' of nearly six weeks, and all the incredible doctors who had taken care of us, but there was no time to think as we carefully manoeuvred John from his wheelchair into the taxi and drove away, waving as we did with thumb and forefinger in a heart shape – the Vietnamese way of sending love. I'd had no word from Kathy.

When we arrived at the airport we gave Vinnie a big tip. He had missed out on all of the tips we would have given him had we not ended up at the hospital instead of enjoying our holiday. I hurried to check us in – the airport was completely empty, apart from an official from the UK embassy, the ambassador, I think. Vinnie insisted on coming with me. When I showed our e-tickets I was told I needed to pay a fine as we had outstayed our visas. Thanks, Kathy, for sorting that. Vinnie took me to another desk and pleaded with the man not to charge us. Whatever Vinnie said to him did the trick, and our papers got stamped to say all clear.

We said goodbye to Vinnie, and I thanked him with tears in my eyes before we went through to passport control. Just before we went through we were stopped by the official from the embassy who had come to say goodbye. He told us we had been upgraded to business class. John looked utterly bewildered by what was happening as we went through passport control, with me pushing his wheelchair. "Not long now," I said to him, "and we can have a large glass of red…" I was absolutely drained and could not wait to get on that plane.

When we boarded, all the crew were in white space suits. We were told we were in premium economy. The crew had been allocated business class as they'd flown in from Cambodia. Every single one of the passengers was wearing a mask, including a baby.

We took off in the darkness. There was no crew to be seen. Eventually someone came out to us in full space suit and rapidly handed out brown paper bags before disappearing. I felt we were flying to space not the UK! I eagerly opened it. I was starving hungry and very thirsty. The bag contained an anaemic bread roll, a miniature piece of cheese the size of a two penny piece, and a single bottle of water. On approach to landing we were handed another brown paper bag with the same contents, the only difference being an added chocolate bar. This was all we were given for the entire 13-hour flight. And no large glass of red wine…

We were so tired, and I was constantly worried about John. I gave him all his meds and injections during the flight, which brought back all my lovely memories of nursing but was so worrying in these circumstances. I constantly checked his temperature, which was high, but not dangerously. I just prayed he would make it through landing and through all the checks at Heathrow – there were bound to be many checks bearing in mind where we had just come from, and the fact the UK cases and deaths were so high – and held his hand and reassured him, trying to keep his spirits up (and mine).

Thursday 13 April

Finally we landed. We waited forever for a wheelchair and eventually arrived at border control. The airport was almost empty, but then we were last off the plane. I noticed two pretty female staff standing around, with no masks on, and asked them why they weren't wearing them. They said they had been told not to as it looked "unprofessional". To be honest, I did not believe them.

When we entered border control there were two police officers standing side by side –and again with no masks on. Again I asked why, and was once more told: "We are not allowed to as it looks unprofessional." So it was true?

Welcome to the UK.

We had just travelled from a country supposedly not as sophisticated as the UK, whose government had acted promptly to halt the spread of the virus and which had (as yet) no deaths, and here we were in England with its lackadaisical attitude. What was going on? No wonder there had been thousands of cases and so many deaths! I couldn't believe what I was hearing. John was too tired to comment.

It was such a relief to see Sam and Jess waiting for us, and they'd bought a whole load of goodies for us to eat in the car. After everything that had happened in the last six weeks, and certainly in the last 24 hours, I was too stunned and tired to think or eat and just stared out at the green English landscape like it was alien to me. All I remember thinking was I hoped the tides would be right for us to get across the Strood to our lovely little island home.

When we got back Sam handed me a huge gin and tonic. As I gulped at it, so relieved to be home and, I admit, so desperate for that drink, I thought about Mum handing me the same drink so long ago when I was visiting her in Wales. She was looking after a friend, Lady Olwyn, and my friend Bill was with me after a sailing trip we had been on. Bill was looking at the large Edwardian picture of Lloyd George – the prime minister from 1916-1922 – on the wall in her sitting room. "Who's that man?" he'd asked, half spluttering on the strength of his gin and tonic. "Oh, Lloyd George was my father," my mother's friend said, and gin squirted from our mouths as if from water pistols as we burst into hysterics! Lady Olwyn had lived at number 10 Downing Street for a while when her father, Lloyd George, was the prime minister, and 'Lloyd George Knew My Father' was 20th Century English school boy folk song. The memory made me smile, and

I finished my huge gin and tonic and had another whilst John was tucked up in bed absolutely exhausted!

I woke up to a welcome hangover and opened a text from Dr Khiem to say John had a dangerous bacteria in his urine and must see a doctor immediately. And so the saga continued. After many phone calls to the local surgery, more antibiotics, a 999 call, two more weeks in isolation and a spell in hospital it was discovered that John had contracted a bacterial infection (worse than MRSA) that is only found overseas. John needed intravenous infusions again, and had a very high temperature. We managed to see a wonderful consultant who insisted on an MRI scan which identified a large abscess on John's prostate. If this had not been diagnosed it would have most likely burst and septicaemia would have occurred… and all the care from the doctors and nurses in Vietnam would have been in vain.

Back in the hands of our incredible NHS, John finally started to recover and, aside from permanent (further) damage to his already damaged lungs, he began to feel like his old self again.

I started to feel more like me too. I have had only one bout of breathing problems, which was dealt with by high dose of steroids. We both knew our close shave with death at the hands of the virus had changed us.

EPILOGUE

I was ridiculed in the UK for weeks for wearing a mask in supermarkets. I often wished I had pushed the media to understand how well Vietnam had handled the pandemic, but then the media weren't listening anyway, as they had their instructions from a government too slow to catch a cold, but as for a virus. . .

To date (of writing) there have been 35 deaths in Vietnam, with a population of approximately 97 million. There have been 128,000 in the UK, population approximately 67 million. Apparently the super spreader in seat 5k said no cases had been traced back to her, but a recent report indicates otherwise.[1]

I can't help thinking that if only she had admitted she had been to Italy she would not have been allowed to board the aircraft, and she would not have caused so much chaos in her country, Vietnam. I wonder if she has ever been able to face that truth...the truth has a tendency to emerge, so we'll see.

As a nurse trained to care for people and preserve lives, this has been hard for me to think about. All the people infected, and all the families affected. I have nothing but praise for the doctors, nurses, cleaners and cooks who went well beyond the call of duty by staying in the confines of the hospital for two months or more without seeing their families and doing the best they could in Vietnam.

---

1 https://wwwnc.cdc.gov/eid/article/26/11/20-3299_article

I see myself as a very different person now. Adversity made me start believing in myself more, and that if you want to achieve something then you can do it. I'll end by saying it's up to each individual to be responsible.

Spread happiness, not the virus.

Celebrating life again!

POSTSCRIPT

I have met some amazing, kind people in my life, some of whom are part of hilarious memories. Henry Cooper – the boxer – was my escort on the flower float when I was Miss Jersey during the Battle of Flowers, and I remember discussing with him the trouble I was having with a boyfriend. "Do you want me to hit him?" he asked, to my amusement, thinking a real battle could happen at the Battle of Flowers! And Peter Alliss, the golf commentator, once asked me at the Royal Liverpool Golf Tournament, "Are you enjoying the golf?" to which I replied, "I haven't seen a golf ball yet. I've been too busy enjoying the champagne in the press tent!" Peter said it was the funniest answer he had heard all year!

Some of the kindest people I've ever met are nurses, and they have also been some of the funniest. We always covered for each other, too, like the time I lost the code for the door to the specialised instruments cupboard in the operating theatre on night duty. Thank goodness we did not have any major emergencies that night. We giggled nervously, though, trying to work out what we would do if I could not get the necessary instruments to operate when the surgeon asked for them!

The most memorable, unselfish people I have ever met were the doctors in Hanoi, Vietnam. They saved our lives, without a doubt. It was certainly not the most hilarious time, but it will never be forgotten, and neither will they. I am looking forward to visiting Vietnam again and seeing those very special people, and my son who I have now not seen for three years.

Life is full of what ifs and risks, and I will continue to take them as that's what makes my love of and the gift of life such fun.

If we had not boarded that plane we would not have got the virus, but the positive thing to take from it is that it made us stronger in ourselves and as a couple, and we witnessed the strength of the Vietnamese people.

If I had accepted a dinner date when the King of Jordan landed his helicopter on the beach next to me when I was sunbathing in the 1970s, how my life could have been so unbelievably different.

If I had pursued my love of go-karting and lived a life in an even faster lane, like Christian Horner, the principal of the Red Bull Formula One Racing Team (who I met at Goodwood), who knows where I would have ended up?

The WHEEL…keeps on turning, but that is another story!

Printed in Great Britain
by Amazon